The Last Shot

City Streets,
Basketball Dreams

DARCY FREY

A MARINER BOOK
Houghton Mifflin Company
BOSTON   NEW YORK

In memory of my father
ROBERT FRANKLIN FREY

First Mariner Books edition 2004
Copyright © 1994 by Darcy Frey
Afterword copyright © 2004 by Darcy Frey

Library of Congress Cataloging-in-Publication Data
Frey, Darcy.
  The last shot : city streets, basketball dreams / Darcy Frey.
    p. cm.
  ISBN 0-395-59770-6
  ISBN 0-618-44671-0 (pbk.)
    1. Basketball — Social aspects — New York (N.Y.) 2. Youth —
  New York (N.Y.) — Recreation. 3. Abraham Lincoln High School
  (New York, N.Y.) — Basketball.   I. Title.
  [GV885.73.N4F74   1996]
  796.323'62'0974723 — dc20
        95-34632

Book design by Melodie Wertelet

Printed in the United States of America

QUM 10 9 8 7 6 5 4 3 2 1

Portions of this book appeared, in different form,
in *Harper's Magazine* and *Details*.

Author's note: This is a work of nonfiction. I have
changed the names of Russell Thomas and his mother.

Prologue

RUSSELL THOMAS places the toe of his right sneaker one inch behind the three-point line. Inspecting the basket with a level gaze, he bends twice at the knees, raises the ball to shoot, then suddenly looks around. What is it? Has he spotted me, watching from the opposite end of the playground? No, something else is up. He's lifting his nose to the wind like a spaniel; he appears to be gauging air currents. Russell waits until the wind settles, bits of trash feathering lightly to the ground. Then he sends a twenty-five-foot jump shot arcing through the soft summer twilight. It drops without a sound through the dead center of the bare iron rim. So does the next one. So does the one after that. Alone in the gathering dusk, Russell begins to work the perimeter against imaginary defenders, unspooling jump shots from all points.

It's the summer of 1991, and Russell has just finished his junior year at Abraham Lincoln High School in Coney Island, New York. Eighteen years old, he stands six feet two, weighs a hundred and eighty pounds, and is the proud owner of a newly shaved scalp and a small goatee. When he practices at this court, everything between his shiny bald top and his jutting, bearded chin goes blank, and he moves over the asphalt as if in a trance — silent, monklike, in a galaxy of his own. Most summer evenings I come by this court to watch Russell and his friends play ball, and I have found few sights quite as stirring as that of Russell's jumper, tracing a meteor curve in the still, expectant air. But the shot, I realize tonight, is merely the final gesture, the public flourish of a private regimen that brings Russell to this court day and night. Avoiding pickup games, he gets down to work: an hour of three-point shooting, then wind sprints up the fourteen flights in his project stairwell, then back to this court where, much to his friends' amusement, he shoots one-handers ten feet from the basket while sitting in a chair.

At this hour Russell usually has the court to himself. Lately New York City has been slogging through one of its enervating heat waves, a string of 95-degree days, and most of Coney Island's other players won't come out until after dark, when the thick, humid air begins to stir with night breezes and the court lights come on. But tonight is turning out to be a fine one — cool and foggy. The low, slanting sun sheds a pink light over the silvery Atlantic just a block away, and milky sheets of fog roll off the ocean and drift in tatters along the project walkways. The air smells of sewage and salt water. At the far end of the court, where someone has torn a hole in the chain-link fence, other players climb in and begin warming up.

"Just do it, right?" I glance to my left, and there is Corey Johnson, smiling mischievously, eyes alight. He nods toward the court — Russell at one end, a group of players stretching out and taking lay-ups at the other — and it does, in fact, resemble a sneaker commercial. "Work hard, play hard, buy yourself a pair of Nikes, young man," Corey intones. Corey, who is known throughout Coney Island for a variety of talents, practices some deft mimicry, and his rendition of a white, stentorian-voiced TV announcer is easily among his best. "They get you where you want to go, which is out of the ghet-to!" He laughs, we shake hands, and he takes up an observation post by my side.

I am always pleased, though somewhat surprised, when Corey comes by this court. Corey is Russell's best friend and one of Lincoln High's other star juniors. But he specializes in ironic detachment and normally shows up courtside, carrying his Walkman, merely to watch for girls with his handsome, hooded eyes. That may be his intention yet. Tonight he is wearing a fresh white T-shirt, expertly ripped along the back and sleeves to reveal glimpses of his sculpted physique, denim shorts that reach to his knees, and a pair of orange sneakers that go splendidly with his lid — a tan baseball cap with orange piping, which he wears with the bill pointing skyward. From his headphones come the sounds of Color Me Badd, and Corey sings along: *I-wanna-sex-you-up* . . . He loops his fingers around the chain-link fence and says, "I tell you, Coney Island is like a disease — of the mind. It makes you lazy. You relax too much. 'Cause all you ever see is other guys relaxing."

There was a time, of course, when Coney Island inspired among its residents more sanguine remarks — when the neighborhood was home to three world-renowned amusement parks, and its streets were lined with three-story homes, filled to the eaves with Jewish, Irish, and Italian families who proclaimed Coney Island the most welcoming place in America for a newly arrived immigrant — a latterday Plymouth Rock. Now, however, all but a few scattered rides have been dismantled; most of the cottages and tripledeckers have succumbed to the bulldozers of urban renewal; and in their place the city has erected a vast tract of housing projects, home to Coney Island's newest arrivals — African-Americans — and packed so densely along a twenty-block stretch that a new skyline has risen at land's end by the beach and the boardwalk.

The experiment of public housing, which has worked throughout the country to isolate its impoverished and predominantly black tenants from the hearts of their cities, may have succeeded here with even greater efficiency because of Coney Island's utter remoteness. On this peninsula, at the southern tip of Brooklyn, there are almost no stores, no trees, no police; nothing, in fact, but block after block of gray-cement projects — hulking, prisonlike, and jutting straight into the sea. Most summer nights now, an amorphous unease settles over Coney Island, as apartments become stifling and the streets fall prey to the gangs and drug dealers. Options are limited: to the south is the stiff gray meringue of the Atlantic; to the north, more than ten miles away, one can just make out the Statue of Liberty and the glass-and-steel spires of Manhattan's financial district. Officially, Coney Island is part of the endless phantasmagoria that is New York City. But on a night like this, as the dealers set up their drug marts in the streets and alleyways, and the sounds of sirens and gunfire keep pace with the darkening sky, it feels like the end of the world.

Yet even in Coney Island there is a use to which a young man's talent, ambition, and desire to stay out of harm's way may be put: there is basketball. Hidden behind the projects are dozens of courts, and every night they fill with restless teenagers, who remain there for hours until exhaustion or the hoodlums take over. The high school dropouts and the aging players who never made it to college usually show up for a physical game at a barren strip of courts by the water known as Chop-Chop Land, where bruises and minutes played are accrued at a one-to-one ratio. The younger kids congregate for rowdy games at Run-and-Gun Land. The court there is short and the rims are low, so everyone can dunk, and the only pass ever made is the one inbounding the ball. At Run-and-Gun, players stay on the move for another reason: the court sits just below one of the most dreaded projects, where Coney Island's worst hoodlums sometimes pass a summer evening "getting hectic," as they say — shooting at each other or tossing batteries and beer bottles onto the court from apartment windows fifteen stories above.

The neighborhood's best players — Russell, Corey, and their brethren on the Lincoln varsity — practice a disciplined, team-driven style of basketball at the court where I am standing tonight, which has been dubbed the Garden, after the New York Knicks' arena. In a neighborhood ravaged by the commerce of drugs, the Garden offers a cherished sanctuary. A few years ago community activists petitioned the housing authority to install night lights. And the players themselves resurfaced the court and put up regulation-height rims that snap back after a player dunks. Russell may be the only kid at the Garden who shoots one-handers from a chair or practices his defensive footwork with a ten-pound brick in each hand, but no one here treats the game as child's play. Even the dealers and hoodlums refrain from vandalizing the Garden, because in Coney Island the possibility of transcendence through basketball — in this case, an athletic scholarship to a four-year Division I college — is an article of faith.

Although a pickup game has begun at the basket nearest Corey and me, Russell still commands the other. As the last light drains from the summer sky, he finishes with three-pointers and moves on to baby hooks: fifteen with the left hand, fifteen with the right; miss one and start all over again. It is not too much to say that basketball has saved Russell. The Thomases — Russell, his mother, and his two younger sisters — live in one of the neighborhood's toughest projects, just a block from this court; and in earlier days Russell often caused his family considerable grief, sometimes leaving home for long stretches to hang out on the streets with his friends. Every teenager does this to some extent, but the custom posed a greater threat in Russell's case since certain of his friends back then liked to wander over to neighboring Brighton Beach in order to hold up pensioners at gunpoint. But having watched so many of his contemporaries fall into gangs or prison or an early grave,

Russell has developed new ambitions for himself. A few months ago, he led the team at Lincoln High to the New York City public school championship, which was played at Madison Square Garden and broadcast citywide on cable TV. For most of his teammates, it was a moment to savor; Russell hardly broke stride to celebrate. Until he wins his college scholarship, sometime in the months ahead, all else in his life seems to dwindle to the vanishing point — everything besides the ball, this basket, and his conviction that, by practicing each day and playing by all the rules, he has set himself on a path that will change his life. "Man, I *hate* Coney Island," Russell has told me several times. "Maybe after I finish college I'll come back to get my mom. But that's it. I'm leaving. And I'm *never* coming back."

Soon the orange court lights at the Garden come on, displacing the encroaching darkness, and two players on either end of the court climb the fence and sit atop the backboards, hanging nets — a sign that a serious game is about to begin. A few minutes later, a uniformed referee actually shows up to officiate. Suddenly a ferocious grinding noise fills the air. It gets louder and louder, and then a teenage kid riding a Big Wheel careers onto the court. He darts through the playground crowd, leaving a wake of pissed-off players, hops off his ride, and watches it crash kamikaze-style into the fence. "Ah, yes, Stephon Marbury," Corey remarks dryly. "Future of the neighborhood."

Stephon is barely fourteen, has yet to begin his freshman year at Lincoln High, but is already considered the most gifted young New York City guard since Kenny Anderson came out of the Lefrak City projects in Queens two years ago on his way to becoming the star of the New Jersey Nets. Last summer, as an eighth-grader, Stephon snuck into a basketball camp for high-schoolers and would have been kicked out, except that he played with such consummate brilliance that his stunt was written up in the sports pages of the *New York Daily News.* Fourteen years old, and his college recruiting has already begun. Coaches send him letters (in violation of NCAA rules), requesting the pleasure of his company during his years of college eligibility; street agents, paid under the table by colleges to bring top players to their programs, are cultivating Stephon; and practically every high school coach in the city heaps him with free gear — sneakers, caps, bags — in an attempt to lure him to his school.

At first glance, Stephon doesn't look like the future of anything. He's diminutive, barely five feet nine, with the rounded forehead and delicate features of an infant. He sports a stylish razor cut and a newly pierced ear, and the huge gold stud seems to tilt his tiny bald head off its axis. Caught somewhere between puberty and superstardom, he walks around with his sneakers untied, the ends of his belt drooping suggestively from his pants, and half a Snickers bar extruding from his mouth. But what on earth is this? Dribbling by himself in a corner of the court, Stephon has raised a ball with one hand directly over his head and threaded it through his legs. From back to front. Without interrupting his dribble. Now he's doing it with *two* balls!

With Stephon here, Corey hands me his Walkman and strolls onto the court. Russell, too, is persuaded to give up his solo regimen and puts his gold chain around my neck for safekeeping. In fact, every star from Lincoln High has come out tonight except the team's center, Tchaka Shipp, but the game won't be delayed on his account. Tchaka lives miles away in the more working-class environs of Jamaica, Queens; and although at six feet seven he towers above all his teammates, he has been leery of hanging around the Coney Island courts ever since he came here to play, spent the night at Corey's apartment, and someone blew up a car right outside Corey's window. Not long ago Tchaka ventured to the Garden, knowing he'd get the best run in all five boroughs here, but after he surveyed the mangy dogs and ragged street people lingering around the court's edges, he concluded, "Too many low-life, rowdy-ass Brooklyn niggers. I'm heading back to Queens. *Now.*"

Tonight, however, darkness brings only a cool, vaporous sea breeze and nothing to distract the players from their game. Basketball, it is commonly said, is a sport of pure instinct, but the five-on-five contest that begins here is something else. Corey and Stephon are cousins, and Russell is as good as family — the three of them have played together since they were in grade school. They seem to move as if the spontaneous, magical geometry of the game has all been rehearsed in advance. Stephon, the smallest by far, is doing tricks with the ball as though it were dangling from his hand by a string, then gunning it to his older teammates with a series of virtuoso no-look passes: behind-the-back passes, sidearm passes, shovel passes. Corey is lulling defenders with his sleepy eyes, then exploding to the basket, where he casually tosses the ball through the hoop. Russell is sinking twenty-footers as if they were six-inch putts.

The game has just begun when a crowd starts to form: sidelined players, three deep, waiting their turn. A prostitute trolling for clients. A drunk yelling maniacally, "I played with Jordan, I played with Jabbar. They ain't *shit.* And neither are *you!*" A buffed-out guy in a silk suit and alligator shoes arrives, swigging from a bottle of Courvoisier. An agent? A scout? The crowd gives him elbow room. A couple of teenage mothers with strollers come by. There are many of them in Coney Island; they get significantly less elbow room.

It's past midnight now, and the ambient glow of Manhattan's remote skyscrapers has turned the sky a metallic blue. Standing courtside, we can see only the darkened outlines of the projects, looming in every direction, and the shirtless players streaking back and forth, drenched in orange light. Now and then the ref steps out from the darkness onto center court and his official stripes glow incongruously beneath the court lights as the Doppler wail of police sirens drifts in from the nearby streets. Corey, sprinting down-court, calls out, "Homeboy! Homeboy!" Standing under his own basket, Stephon lets fly with a long, improbable pass that Corey, running full speed, somehow manages to catch and dunk in one balletic leap. The game is called on account of total pandemonium: players and spectators are screaming and staggering around the court — knees buckling, heads held in astonishment. Even Mr. Courvoisier loses his cool. Stephon laughs and points to the rim, still shuddering from its run-in with Corey's fists. "Yo, cuz!" he yells. "Make it bleed!" Then he raises his arms jubilantly and dances a little jig, rendered momentarily insane by the sheer, giddy pleasure of playing this game to perfection.

The
Summer
Season

One

ABRAHAM LINCOLN HIGH SCHOOL is a massive yellow brick building of ornate stonework and steel-gated windows at the end of Ocean Parkway, a stately, tree-lined boulevard about a mile from the Coney Island projects. Built in 1930, in the grand style of public architecture, Lincoln once counted itself among the top academic high schools in New York, its student body filled with the sons and daughters of the immigrants who had arrived in the neighbor-' hood at the turn of this century. But as Coney Island has deteriorated over the years, so has Lincoln High. Directly across Ocean Parkway from the school are Brighton Beach and several other Jewish neighborhoods; but the kids from those areas are often sent elsewhere for their education, as Lincoln has become, little by little, a ghetto school for the projects.

Lincoln is by no means the worst or most dangerous of New York's almost two hundred public high schools. That distinction is shared by Thomas Jefferson in Brooklyn, where two students were recently gunned down in the hallway as they walked to class; William Taft in the Bronx, where kids occasionally throw M-80s into crowded classrooms; and the forty-five other schools throughout the five boroughs where metal detectors have been installed at the front doors to separate students from their coat-pocket arsenals. The faculty at Lincoln includes some of the most dedicated teachers in the city, as well as a principal who just retired after twenty-two years of holding the school together through this era of enormous change. Still, a malaise has set in at Lincoln, as it has at so many inner-city schools. Twenty-five hundred students attend Lincoln, packing every inch of its yellow-walled corridors at dismissal time, and it often seems that an equal number of security guards is required to keep them from inflicting grievous bodily harm on one another. The first day I dropped by, in the spring of 1991, there was much commotion in the Lincoln hallway because the locker of a student was found to contain a handgun. On my second visit, the weapon in question was a six-inch knife. After one student was taken by ambulance to Coney Island Hospital with a neck wound requiring forty stitches, even some of the most peaceable kids at the school began carrying X-Acto knives for protection.

Most of the African-American students at Lincoln arrive each morning from the nine subsidized housing complexes that run from West Twenty-first Street in Coney Island to West Thirty-seventh, and between Neptune Avenue and Surf — a thirty-block grid of streets comprising not much more than project buildings and basketball courts. Many of the students' parents are jobless and support their families with welfare and food stamps. Although the universal teenage fashion of baseball caps and baggy, low-riding jeans provides a certain camouflage, the overwhelming poverty of these families is evident in the Lincoln corridors, where kids sometimes show up for school in midwinter wearing nothing but hooded sweatshirts, huddling close to hallway radiators to keep warm; or at the end of each school year when a handful of seniors who cannot afford the school's $88 cap-and-gown fee apply for special dispensation. A lot of Lincoln kids remain in the neighborhood after they graduate, working as orderlies at Coney Island Hospital or store managers at McDonald's or foremen on construction crews — jobs not much better than the ones their parents have, if indeed their parents have any jobs at all.

Amid such diminished prospects, the opportunities presented to those kids who make the school's varsity basketball team are stunningly vast — a door in a constricted room suddenly flung open on the wider world. Filling its rosters with kids who, in a grim bit of humor, call their court the Garden, though they must share it each day with the neighborhood's prostitutes and junkies, the Lincoln team has become the odds-on favorite each year to play for the city championship at the real Madison Square Garden, under television lights and the gaze of six thousand fans. And Lincoln's reputation as New York's best public school team is now drawing invitations to national tournaments, allowing kids who have never lived anywhere but the Coney Island projects to find themselves on week-long, all-expenses-paid trips to Florida, Las Vegas, and San Diego.

But city championships and national tournaments, however thrilling, are transient moments. The ultimate reward of making the varsity squad arrives in the form of the dozens of college coaches who visit Lincoln each year with the promise of full, four-year athletic scholarships to schools like Seton Hall, Providence, Temple, Syracuse, and Villanova. Every year they come — descending upon this forgotten corner of New York to take the measure of the school's best players. You can always tell when a college coach has entered the crowded Lincoln gym for a game: the long wooden bleachers have already begun to fill — with hopeful parents, older brothers curious to check out the new crew, kids from the junior varsity studying the moves of the upperclassmen. Everyone in Coney Island reads the high school sports section in *New York Newsday* to size up Lincoln's competition in the city's Public School Athletic League (the PSAL); and for every crucial home game the neighborhood packs the house, streaming into the Lincoln gym until the door monitors stanch the flood and the refs tell everyone to "take a couple of big steps back from the court now, or we're not gonna start this game." And just at that moment, before the ref walks to center court and the ball goes up, a famous coach — P. J. Carlesimo from Seton Hall or Rollie Massimino of Villanova — will appear at the door, and the news will ripple through the raucous crowd, already decked out in Seton Hall caps and Villanova sweatshirts in anticipation of a moment like this.

Out on the court, the players fight the urge not to eyeball the new arrivals; etiquette requires a cool indifference. But the presence of the suits amid the Afros, flattops, and box-and-fades in the Lincoln bleachers is unquestionably momentous. For the prospect of being recruited by a top college coach offers a Lincoln student more than the opportunity to play NCAA ball for four years in front of millions of viewers on ESPN. It promises something substantial and long-lasting: that even if an NBA contract isn't in the cards for any of the players, their talent and tenacity on the court will at least reward them with a free college education, a decent job after graduation, and a one-way ticket out of Coney Island — a chance, in other words, to liberate themselves from the grinding daily privations of life in the ghetto once and for all.

Coaches were everywhere at Lincoln during the spring following the team's 1991 city championship. Russell, Corey, and Tchaka were finishing their junior year, and Stephon was expected to join them as a freshman in the fall. Winning a championship at any time during his high school career gives a player a tremendous boost toward college recruitment. That Russell, Corey, and Tchaka had won their titles as juniors seemed even more auspicious. Now that the National Collegiate Athletic Association, the governing body of college athletics, allows high school players to sign with colleges in the fall of their senior year, most coaches pick the promising juniors and watch them play during July and August, when the nation's best players go head to head at the summer basketball camps. Then the coaches start recruiting as soon as the players return to school in the fall.

It was a fine time to have caught up with the Lincoln varsity. Celebrations of the team's 55–40 victory over South Shore High School at Madison Square Garden kept going off throughout the spring, like intermittent explosions after the Fourth. The New York City Board of Education awarded each Lincoln player a wristwatch with PSAL 1991 and a tiny basketball printed on the dial. *Newsday*, which had covered the team all season, presented the players with a blue-cloth championship banner, which they hung from the rafters of the Lincoln gym. Rick Barnes, the head coach at Providence College, even made a surprise appearance at the team's end-of-the-year dinner to deliver a speech about pride, discipline, and the pot of gold at the end of the rainbow. And that, it seemed, was no exaggeration. The current mania for basketball in this country — which one sees on NBA broadcasts, during the NCAA's "March Madness" tournament, even on sneaker commercials selling the work ethic along with those $120 high-tops — has translated into extraordinary opportunities for players like Russell, Corey, Tchaka, and Stephon. In the next eight months, if everything goes as it should, these players will be offered the chance — so rare under any circumstances, but especially rare in a place like Coney Island — to change irrevocably the course of their lives just as they are coming into adulthood. And having attached myself to the team as its reporter-in-residence, I will be around to watch the whole thing happen.

•

A few more weeks now and the 1991 school year will be over. For the past month the air has been thick with a yellow haze, and with the school windows open you can smell the sharp tang of the Atlantic just a few blocks away. To get to Lincoln from the Coney Island projects, you take a bus or walk down Surf Avenue, which runs parallel with the boardwalk. When you hit Ocean Parkway, you hang a left and walk north a few blocks to the school. If you hang a right, however, you end up on the beach. A lot of Lincoln High is on the beach these days. This is the time of year when the indolent weather turns a student's thoughts toward last-minute truancy, and anyone who is contemplating dropping out is advised by his friends to "just do it."

But Russell, Corey, and Tchaka are all in school, and happily so. There is much still to discuss. There is the continuing postgame analysis of the team's championship at the Garden — more specifically, how *Tchaka kept dunkin' on that skinny-ass nigger from South Shore and Russell was hitting his treys like water — waap, waap, waap* . . . There are those PSAL watches, which are undeniably dorky but do afford the players the pleasure of asking each other, "Yo, what time is it?" so that they can look at their wrists and exclaim, like NBA broadcasters, "It's *championship* time!"

Now that the PSAL season is over, the players are free to go home right after school. But even after the last class bell rings, disgorging hundreds of students into the school corridors, they always gather outside the gym for some last-minute foolishness and often an impromptu meeting with their coach. And here comes Tchaka Shipp now, considerably more relaxed than he looked the other day out by the projects, loping down the corridor like Magic Johnson — head and neck stretched forward and the rest of his body in hot pursuit. *Tchaka* is short for *Tchaka Omowale*, an African name meaning "the king-child has come home." And one must concede the point: the name is actually beginning to fit. Not yet seventeen and already six feet seven, Tchaka is a majestic-looking kid, with high cheekbones and a long sloping forehead that lend him an Egyptian aspect, though the gold-rimmed glasses he occasionally favors tilt his image more toward Sidney Poitier. Today he is wearing long plaid shorts and a tight-fitting tank top, and with his imposing rack of shoulder muscles straining the seams of his shirt he seems to rise above the noisy crowd in the hallway like a parade float.

"Yo!" Tchaka yells in my direction. "Yo!"

"What's up?"

"Couple more weeks I'm *outta* here!" he cries. "Takin' my six-seven self to Nike!"

This upcoming trip to "Nike" is, not to put too fine a point on it, precisely what Tchaka has been dreaming of every day for the past year. Each summer the Nike sneaker company invites the nation's 120 finest high school basketball players to Indianapolis for a week-long, all-expenses-paid jamboree. Also in attendance is every top Division I college coach in America, there to appraise the talent and reward the best. Ever since he received his invitation, Tchaka has been in an expansive mood, and today is no exception. He walks up to me in the corridor and claps me on the shoulder. But immediately his eyes grow large and he brings his hand to his mouth. "You know what this means, don't you? There are going to be at least thirty guys my size or taller! I'm gonna be the little one!"

That will require no small adjustment on Tchaka's part. For two years now, Tchaka has had his way with the PSAL as he established his front-court game — maximum use of elbows on the boards and an insatiable appetite for the ball. From time to time last season Tchaka would receive a pass at the foul line, allow himself a single dribble, and with his uncommon leaping ability find himself eye to eye with the rim for an easy lay-up or dunk. But he soon discovered it was also possible to cry out like some herniated weight lifter, ream the ball through the hoop, and then, as he hung from the rim with a fiendish look, listen for the urgent, swelling, seashell roar of the crowd rushing in from the bleachers, howling their delight. "One more second on the rim, young man, and you've got yourself a technical," the ref would warn as soon as Tchaka had landed on the firm earth. But Tchaka would grin and shake his head and point out — most reasonably, in light of the still-whooping fans — that monster dunks were precisely what the crowd came to see. Tchaka sometimes concludes his games by collapsing flat on his back at center court, an expression of spent bliss on his face and his shorts split violently up the seam.

But that was the PSAL and among the Lilliputians. How Tchaka will fare at Nike, against the nation's best and biggest players, remains an open question. Despite his size, Tchaka comes to the game with certain disadvantages, not the least of which is that he grew up in slightly less constricted circumstances than his Coney Island teammates. Unlike Russell, Corey, and Stephon, whose recreational options in the projects were limited to either basketball or basketball, Tchaka's preferred sport until he became a high school freshman was bicycling. But having suddenly elongated to six feet three, Tchaka found his knees scraping the handlebars, and he swapped his bike for his first pair of high-tops. Three years later he was still growing, almost visibly to the naked eye, and playing at times with some awkwardness, as if he had rented his body on game day and got stuck with a size too big. As a sophomore, Tchaka averaged only four points per game; now, as a junior, ten. He has trouble shooting a jumper more than eight feet from the basket and sometimes can't catch a pass unless it hits him squarely in the chest. Walking down the street, Tchaka sometimes dribbles a phantom ball through his legs and behind his back, since the genuine article often ties him up in knots.

Frustrated by this gap between his real and imagined games, these days Tchaka has initiated a rigorous program of self-improvement. When he isn't in school or on the court, he is usually in his bedroom in Jamaica, studying college games on tape. Tchaka has hundreds of them, and most evenings when he gets home from school his first order of business is to fish through the pile for a vintage contest — UNLV v. Seton Hall, perhaps — pop it in his VCR, and lie on his bed for the next two hours, analyzing the Running Rebels' power moves to the basket.

Now in the crowded Lincoln corridor, standing chest-deep in the moving tide of homebound students, Tchaka shows me what his research has yielded: a technique, when you've been boxed out for a rebound, to spin around your opponent in order to re-establish position. One of Tchaka's classmates, walking down the corridor with her school-books clasped to her chest, tries to get position on *him*, yelling, "Come on, Tchaka, get out of my way!" But Tchaka is focused elsewhere, planting his sneakers on the marble floor and executing perfect spin moves, one after another, in a dizzying pirouette. "Gonna have to try this one at Nike!" he says.

I feel a pair of eyes on us and quickly spot Russell Thomas over in the corner, watching Tchaka's maneuvers. Russell, I know, would like to be going to Nike himself, and feels that he should be, given all his hours of solitary drillwork at the Garden. Tchaka may be the team's tallest player, but it was Russell, by virtue of his extraordinary self-imposed discipline, who got the ball last season whenever the game was on the line. During competition, Russell's concentration level is so high that it actually comes as a surprise to see him miss. His ability to drop one jump shot after another into the hoop has earned him the nickname Tick Tick, because he scores like clockwork — though it could also refer to the fact that he often seems like a device about to go off. That, more or less, is the way Russell looks now: as he listens to Tchaka discussing his Nike plans, a deep crease forms between his eyebrows and his features settle into a fierce mask. Only his eyes are in motion.

Of all the Lincoln players, Russell has perhaps the most difficult home life, living as he does in one of Coney Island's worst projects; and the promise that a college scholarship could release him from that life often brings him not only hope, but also a considerable amount of anxiety when he begins to doubt the certainty of this means of escape. The pressure that puts on him can affect his behavior, often in mysterious ways. One time after a recent game, for example, Russell snuck out the back door of the locker room to avoid a team meeting, leaving everyone wondering whether he was angry at himself for his performance or angry at his teammates for not passing him the ball. Probably both. A few weeks later he skipped the team's year-end dinner, apparently angry that he hadn't been named the season's Most Valuable Player. (The award went to a graduating senior.) Russell's anxiety took a more serious turn last fall. Not long after the start of the school year, he got into a violent fight with his girlfriend. Terrified — quite irrationally — that he might get thrown in jail and never be recruited to college, Russell climbed to the top of one of Coney Island's highest buildings. It took almost half an hour of reasoned talk by his high school coach and members of the Sixtieth Precinct to bring him back from the edge.

Since that day, however, Russell has vowed to change, and he has in many ways. Although schoolwork has never come as easily to him as it does to Tchaka, this year Russell is determined to let nothing — not a low school average nor a poor SAT score — prevent him from qualifying for Division I ball and earning his bachelor's degree. According to NCAA rules, students who want to play sports at four-year Division I schools — those with the nation's top athletic programs — may do so only after maintaining at least a 70 average in high school and receiving a combined score of 700 on the math and verbal sections of the SATs. This year, Russell has given up his lunch period to study, and lately he's been carrying around a set of vocabulary flash cards, which he pulls out whenever there isn't a basketball in his hands.

Nevertheless, Russell can't always suppress the envy he feels when he sees good grades or Nike invitations fall into Tchaka's hands. And Tchaka, for his part, continues to think of Russell as a bit of a "head case," a kid with "social problems." So when Russell walks up to Tchaka in the school corridor now, Tchaka tilts his head back an inch or two, almost as if he were expecting to get punched. Russell extends his hand. "Yo, Tchak — I heard the news about Nike," he says. "I'm proud of you, man." They shake solemnly, and Russell tells me that he'll be making appearances this summer at the B/C All-Stars basketball camp in Pennsylvania, as well as the Empire State Games in Albany, New York. These venues are not quite as prestigious as Nike — in a game that rewards height, Russell stands only six feet two — but they are still fine opportunities to gain exposure in front of the college coaches. "Besides that, I guess I'll just work out alone and study for my SATs." Russell lowers his gaze, contemplating his sneakers. "I got some good news too," he says, hesitantly. Still looking down, he pulls from his back pocket a piece of paper and presents it to Tchaka. Unfolding it, Tchaka discovers he is holding Russell's report card. Russell glances up at Tchaka. "I did good, huh?"

Tchaka sees that his teammate has just got a 79 — better, for the first time, than himself. "Yeah, Russell!" he cries. "You're a student-athlete now!" Tchaka reaches forward with his giant hand and gives Russell's freshly shaved head a congratulatory rub. Corey Johnson, walking down the corridor, observes this ceremony and joins in polishing Russell's smooth dark orb.

"What are we doing?" Corey asks with a smile. "Making a wish?"

"Russell got a seventy-nine!" Tchaka exclaims while Russell rocks from one foot to the other with glad self-consciousness. "Let's see *your* report card," Tchaka says meaningfully, but Corey has taken a step backward and begun shimmying across the corridor, rapping something to himself while several (female) classmates look on. Whether he's hanging out by the Coney Island courts or around the Lincoln corridor, Corey always cuts a stylish figure. The other day he showed up in school wearing a hoop earring, gold toothcaps, and a floppy suede hat, which made him look like a cross between LL Cool J and Joan Baez. Today he's back to long jean shorts and an artfully torn T-shirt. I ask him how he's planning to spend his summer.

"Oh, I'll go to the B/C camp with Russell," Corey replies casually. "But mostly I'll just stay in shape running on the beach. The sand is good for your legs, helps you keep up your stamina. I tell you, mostly I just want some time to relax."

Apparently Corey has gotten a jump on his summer plans, for the word in the corridor today is that he has just relaxed his way to three failed classes and now possesses a 66 average — approximately one failed test away from losing his eligibility to play on the Lincoln team. But Corey doesn't look overly concerned. In fact, he seems to take a certain pleasure in locking himself into Houdini's trunk, then reaching into his bag of tricks for the secret key. That, evidently, is one of his specialties, if the story he begins to tell his friends in the corridor now is any indication. During a recent game, it seems, Corey drove the baseline. Two huge defenders converged on him. Corey had already left the ground when this situation developed, so there was nothing for him to do but twist through his outsized opponents, spinning 360 degrees around, and effortlessly roll the ball off his fingertips into the basket. "I don't know how that happened," Corey says to all of us with mock sincerity. "There was like five seconds left. I got the ball. I looked at it. It said PLEASE SHOOT ME. So I did." He shrugs. Russell and Tchaka burst out laughing. Corey keeps a straight face, though his eyes are smiling at the corners.

"What the hell are you guys so happy about? I haven't seen anything you've done worth getting happy about!" Ah, even Coach Hartstein is in a good mood today. "We gotta have a team meeting," he announces, walking brusquely past his players into an empty classroom. As a coach, Bobby Hartstein is cast against type, and not merely because he is white and Jewish in a predominantly black, inner-city school. Thin, nervous, with tired eyes, a bushy mustache, and a head of hair that brings to mind a plate of baked ziti, Hartstein speaks in a raspy Brooklyn voice; it is an impressive and versatile instrument, and when the standard, red-faced coach-scream doesn't yield results, Hartstein drops to a lower register, shrugging his shoulders and turning his palms to the ceiling in a time-honored Yiddish gesture — the miffed uncle who didn't get invited to the bar mitzvah. "If you're too scared to play," he often tells his players before important games, "just let me know. I'm not gonna get mad. Really. Just let me know. I'll be happy to bench you. What do I care if you end up playing college ball at Yeshiva?" In fact, however, Hartstein — who is also the school's dean of special education — works ceaselessly on behalf of his players, helping them with their schoolwork, driving them home after practice, and grumbling all the way about "how much of my goddamned time these kids take up."

Noisily following their coach into the classroom, Russell, Corey, Tchaka, and their teammates shoehorn themselves into the one-piece desk-and-seat contraptions built over forty years ago for kids half their size. There's much to discuss: report cards, SAT filing deadlines, everyone's summer camp schedules. "First of all," Hartstein begins, "I want to announce that we have a new Mr. High IQ by the name of Russell Thomas, who just got a seventy-nine." While the team gives him a round of applause, Russell smiles and lowers his forehead to his desk. "With grades like that," Hartstein goes on, "you deserve your recruiting mail." This must be welcome news to Russell. College coaches send letters to the Lincoln players care of Hartstein, who locks them away until the players, by getting good report cards and test scores, earn the right to look at them. Last month, after Tchaka came within ten points of a 700 on his first SAT attempt, Hartstein gave him all his recruiting mail; for the past few weeks, Russell has been impatiently awaiting his. "All your mail is in my locker, Russell," Hartstein says. "In fact, you're getting too much. It's starting to annoy me. Come by after the meeting and I'll give it to you."

But now, hearing that it's his for the asking, Russell looks up suddenly. "No, Coach, don't give it to me!" he cries.

"Why not?"

"'Cause I'll stop working hard in class!"

"You sure?"

"Yeah, yeah." Russell, with a pained look, shakes his head. "I won't mean to stop, but I will." Russell may act in inexplicable ways at times, but his constant quest for athletic and academic betterment makes him a joy to coach.

"Okay, suit yourself." Hartstein shrugs and turns his attention to Corey. "Now Corey — hey, Corey! Where the hell is Corey going?" Corey has just sauntered out into the hallway to meet some girls. "This kid fails three classes and he's still screwing around. *Corey!*"

"Just talkin' to my fans," Corey says, calmly rejoining the group.

"This kid is special," Hartstein announces to the team, as if Corey were still in the hallway. "He's extremely bright, but he's lazy. Russell — what did you say to me about Corey?"

"Corey's crazy-smart, Coach. He just don't use it."

"He uses it," Tchaka interjects, raising an eyebrow and running his gold neck chain through his mouth. "Just not in the classroom."

"All right, all right," says Hartstein, moving on to more salutary matters. "The good news, Corey, is you can still avoid spending your summer in summer school." Another round of applause, and Corey looks on with a bemused expression. "The bad news is, not by much. All right, on to topic number one."

"What's that, Coach?"

Hartstein is fishing for something inside his gym bag. "Topic number one is . . ." He can't find what he's looking for. "And I know you're all gonna be pleased when you see it . . ." The players lean forward. "Ah, here it is." Hartstein holds up a sheet of paper. "Our very own design for . . . *championship team jackets!*"

The players begin to clap and hoot. Above the din, Hartstein tries to explain that he commissioned a Lincoln art student to invent a logo to be stitched on the back of each team member's jacket. The student came up with an elaborate design — a cartoon figure perched on a rim, his head shaped like a basketball, and a leering grin on his face. "These are gonna be beautiful," Hartstein says, sounding like a man feigning enthusiasm, though he is in fact as pleased as can be. "Nobody in the city is going to have anything like this. Now, about this angry expression. I think we can probably ask the kid to do another version —" But the players have begun to clap rhythmically, drowning out their coach and approving the design by spontaneous voice vote. "Oh, c'mon, it doesn't even look like he's smiling!" Hartstein protests.

"No, that's the way we want it," Russell insists. "Looks like Tchaka driving the lane: *aaaargh!*"

"You *sure* you guys want the mouth on the side like this? You *sure* you want him scowling?"

"Yeah!"

"It's fly!"

"It's hype!"

"Word!"

"Damn. I gotta walk around with some guy with a stupid grin on my jacket? Okay, it's up to you. You're the champs. It's just that I figured *some*body in this room had taste, but . . . I guess not." Hartstein executes one final shrug, as prelude to his closing remarks. "Now listen up. The next few months may be the most important of your life. If you have any pride, you oughtta bust your ass for the next few weeks in class. Work hard there and on your game, and you can turn a decent college into a good one. A good one into a great one. Tchaka, Russell, Corey — you should all go to Division One schools. I promise you: all the hard work you do this summer will pay off. That's what separates the guys who make it from the ones who don't. This is not fun and games. If you just run up and down all summer in the parks, then two years from now you'll still be in the playground. And it doesn't matter to me. Honestly, I really don't care. You won't be the first to blow it; you won't be the last. I've seen a million kids . . ."

Hartstein goes on like this for a while — telling his players how little he expects of them because he knows how much they expect of themselves. Questioning his players' commitment is Hartstein's best motivational tool, his ace in the hole. Pride on this team, he knows, is rarely in short supply, though he can never predict the moments it may surface. It was there, of course, in the locker room before their games last season, as Tchaka, Corey, Russell, and their teammates crowded toward the door for their big entrance, shuffling themselves into some precise but obscure order that only they understood. ("They think they're the Rockettes," Hartstein once observed.) But to the coach's surprise, it also appeared after the team lost the New York State championship to a team that boasted a 29–0 record during the regular season but featured two players who were rumored to have missed forty classes or more, and one who had been released recently from jail for stabbing another student. "Just shows what kind of a program we're from," Russell announced, looking up from his vocabulary flash cards on the bus ride back to Brooklyn, and his teammates all agreed.

If matters of pride receive special emphasis on this team, it may be because — no matter how sought-after they are by the college coaches or how promising their futures — until the day they pack their bags and leave Coney Island for good, the Lincoln players will live in one of the city's most neglected neighborhoods and operate under a cloud of suspicion wherever they go. At least since the 1982 PSAL playoffs, when an off-duty security guard chased a knife-wielding fan directly onto the court and put a gun to his head while the crowd and players ran, screaming, for the exits, anyone playing in or watching a postseason PSAL game is frisked at the gym door by guards with metal detectors. And then there is that ritual of basketball in the urban public schools: the pregame *passeggiata* of the neighborhood's drug dealers. During warm-ups in certain gyms, the steel doors will swing open, and slowly, conspicuously, daring the security guards to stop them, the dealers will make their entrance, signaling to friends in the bleachers while strolling around the court draped in leather, fur, and several pounds of gold.

Lincoln and almost two thirds of the city's two hundred other public high schools now restrict most games to home fans in order to prevent riots among rival schools and appearances by unsavory characters. Still, despite these precautions, some college coaches write off Lincoln completely, assuming the players are too rowdy and uncoachable, and stand a slim chance of meeting the NCAA's eligibility requirements. If they want to recruit in New York City, they'll go to the parochial schools, which offer safer environments and better academic preparation. And no college coach relishes the thought of making home recruiting visits in the Coney Island projects, walking up darkened, drug-infested stairwells yelling, as some have been known to do, "Coach! I'm a coach! Don't hurt me!"

The widespread expectation that they will behave like thugs and hoodlums is not lost on the Lincoln players. Two years ago, when the team arrived at its hotel for a Christmas tournament in Las Vegas, they found themselves in exile, separated by several floors from the parochial and suburban school players and the hotel's other guests. It was the same story in Philadelphia — although a week after that trip Hartstein received a sheepish letter from the tournament director explaining that he never thought players from a Brooklyn public high school could be such *gentlemen*, and when would they like to come back?

Just a few days ago I had occasion to witness some of the attitudes directed at the Lincoln players when I went to a Manhattan gym to watch Tchaka play with an independent summer-league team, which happens to be all black, against a group of white players visiting from New Jersey. Though he had five inches on the white team's tallest player, Tchaka was struggling to find his game and, as a result, was committing his usual sins of eagerness — traveling, charging, goaltending. Every time the whistle blew on one of Tchaka's transgressions, the crowd let up a carnival cheer. Tchaka hung in there, slapping the ref's ass good-naturedly whenever the offical made a call on him. But the mood in the bleachers, filled predominantly with the relatives of the white players, soon turned ugly. Whenever Tchaka took one step too many on his route to a crushing jam, hecklers would call for a technical, yelling, "This ain't the NBA!" which seemed a euphemism for the resentment many white players feel toward blacks with overwhelming talent, since the NBA is 80 percent black and just about the only arena in which whites are seriously in danger of losing their jobs to blacks. Next to me in the stands sat the father of a New Jersey player who was getting dunked on every time Tchaka charged downcourt. "This monster's still in high school?" said the aggrieved father, assuming that I was related to one of the white New Jersey players. "What is he, a sixth-year student?" Toward the end of the game, Tchaka went to the foul line for two shots. By this time, the crowd was all but pelting him with rotten tomatoes. When Tchaka airballed the first one, the crowd gave him an ovation. "Probably never practiced a foul shot in his life — just runs up and down in the parks," the father observed. Tchaka glanced at me, his expression shot through with panic. Would his hard-won skills desert him *now*, when he needed them not only for the purposes of this game, but also to put one in the face of the hostile crowd? Tchaka locked his eyes on the rim. The next shot, thank God, sailed defiantly through the net.

Sometimes, as I watched Tchaka, Russell, and Corey during my first months with the team, I felt that I had caught up with them at a crucial juncture in their lives. Sports has a way of doing that, of compressing life's many unremarkable days into something heightened and exalted, of kindling hope and auguring great deeds. One feels this around young athletes of all kinds because of the rhythm of winning and losing and the dramatic foreshortening of their careers. But one feels it especially around athletes from neighborhoods like Coney Island, where today they live in projects so menacing that even some of the Lincoln social workers won't make home visits anymore; and tomorrow they may be, if not highly paid professionals, then in all likelihood the first members of their families ever to graduate from a four-year college, the first to find decent employment, the first to take their long-denied place in the mainstream American economy — the game of basketball giving them perhaps their last best chance to do so.

Now as Coach Hartstein concludes his speech, and the team meeting breaks up, and the players get ready for their season of summer ball, the talk turns, as it often does at such moments, to the NBA's college draft. Lately, *Newsday* has been featuring a number of stories about college players like Kenny Anderson, who is about to leave Georgia Tech after his sophomore year, sign a multimillion-dollar NBA contract, and buy his mother a nice big house. "Just think, Russell, a few more years and *we* could be pros," Tchaka says, giving his teammate's back a hearty thump. "Kenny did it." Out of the classroom they file, three in a row, in a flak burst of noise and movement, as Hartstein stands by the door, discreetly handing out bus fare home to the players he knows to be most in need. Never in their lives would they be in possession of so little and on the brink of so much.

Two

TCHAKA and his family live on a quiet, dead-end block of one-story red brick homes in the black, working-class neighborhood of Jamaica, Queens. Tchaka, his older sister, Tracie, and his mother, Annette, moved there from Bedford-Stuyvesant a year ago, after Mrs. Shipp, walking home from a neighbor's house, happened to witness the execution, gangland-style, of two drug dealers on her own front stoop. This was horrifying, and the limits of what the family could bear, but it was by no means unusual. During their years in Bed-Stuy the Shipps often woke at three A.M. to the sound of machine gun fire and shattering glass from the street below, and they grew expert at rolling swiftly beneath their beds, where they would remain, hearts in their throats, until the shooting stopped. Tchaka himself was assaulted one afternoon in Bed-Stuy by a gang of twenty hoodlums. Hopped up and well armed, they caught him just as he was leaving basketball practice and took an immediate interest in his new Reeboks. Unwilling to part with them, Tchaka fled. The hoodlums opened fire down the street. Tchaka heard bullets whizzing past him and braced himself for the impact of one to his spine, but the shooting abruptly ceased. As he rounded a corner, he saw that the parked car of a fearsome neighborhood drug dealer had been hit. When the outraged dealer stood up (he was behind it, polishing his fender), the gang members respectfully held their fire. After a while,

Tchaka's mother began to wish her son — this vessel of all her hopes — had never grown so tall. Being six feet seven once helped to ward off trouble; now, in the era of semiautomatics, it merely presented shooters with a larger target.

The Shipps' exodus to Jamaica did not come without sacrifice. Mrs. Shipp, widowed six years before, when her husband died of pneumonia, works long hours as a secretary at a nearby community college in order to meet the rent, more than twice what the family paid in Bed-Stuy. Tracie, a twenty-four-year-old social worker, dreams of living alone but has agreed to stay at home for the time being, contributing half her salary to family expenses. And Tchaka now lives so far from Lincoln High that he must take three subways and a bus, beginning the hour-and-a-half trip at six A.M., when he is often the only rider on the train. But no one in the Shipp household complains; these are considered light taxes to pay in order to avoid Bed-Stuy or the Coney Island projects. "Out there it's a real jungle," Mrs. Shipp once said to me. "All the young boys are so hyped up — with guns, drugs, gold jewelry, fast cars, loud music, hanging out on corners with their pants down to their knees. Sometimes I see a bit of the street in Tchaka. I tell him, 'Don't bring the street in *my* house! I don't like the street in the *street!*'" She laughed, time and distance from those horrific Bed-Stuy days having given her the ability to do so. "But that's just Tchaka fooling around, or being so street that no one bothers him. Deep down he hates all the riffraff as much as me."

After school let out for the year, I started hanging out with Tchaka in Queens, getting better acquainted with him in anticipation of our joint trip to the Nike camp in early July. We rarely went without company. Because of his height, his good looks, his engaging manner, Tchaka is constantly approached by people — sometimes complete strangers — who ask if he can get them courtside seats to

Knicks games, or offer their opinion on where he should play college ball, or merely inquire what the weather is like up there. "Sunny now, but thunderstorms on the way," Tchaka will say with a pleasant smile. "Better move along — you don't want to get caught in the rain." Often the attention his height attracts is less flattering. After a tournament game in upstate New York, Tchaka was strolling with his teammates through a suburban neighborhood when a policeman suddenly materialized from behind a hedge.

"Looking for trouble?"

Tchaka and his friends came to a halt. For a moment, Tchaka seemed to inflate with anger, dwarfing the stout policeman, who stood blocking his path. These are the moments that keep Annette Shipp suspended at night between waking and sleep, waiting for the reassuring sound of Tchaka's key in the door. Tchaka reached forward with his hand. The cop moved toward his nightstick. Tchaka patted the policeman's shoulder. "Relax, Officer," he said. "*Ree-laax.* We're just going for a walk."

"I'll be watching you," the cop said with a snarl.

"And I'll still be walking," Tchaka replied. ("And cops wonder why they're always getting shot," he muttered to his friends.)

In the world of high school basketball, which brings black inner-city kids into contact with mainstream white society, some for the very first time, there are so many conflicting expectations about how players will or should behave that some kids, if they don't simply withdraw in anger, lapse into a confused and watchful silence when dealing with the white adult world. But Tchaka moves easily among the various social circles into which basketball thrusts him: homeboy on the street; inquisitive student in the classroom; promising college recruit looking, as he says publicly, to "use basketball to further my education" but allowing privately that he hopes one day to "bring back the serious loot in the NBA." Only on the rarest occasions do his wires — so finely tuned to the complex frequencies of race and social class — get crossed, as they did once when he was being interviewed by a sports reporter after a heartbreaking loss. Tchaka was waxing respectful about the skills of his opponent, feeding the writer all the clichés that athletes learn at a remarkably young age to guard against the hazards of candor. "He played a great game . . . You gotta give him credit . . . He kept his poise down the stretch." Then Tchaka gripped the sides of his head, recalling one particular moment in the game just ended. "You see that last play, right before the buzzer? *Word!* That nigger was buggin'! He threw a two-handed tomahawk dunk on me. Cocked that sucker all the way to his *nuts!*" Horrified, Tchaka opened his eyes wide and clapped his hand over his open mouth. "Don't quote me, okay?"

•

On the day that he and I are scheduled to fly to the Nike camp in Indianapolis, however, Tchaka is not feeling his most self-possessed. He woke early, nervous as a cat, unable to sleep. He watched some college games on tape. He drank a couple glasses of strawberry milk, his favorite meal. Then he tried to pack — without much success, by the looks of things when I arrive around noon. A riot of T-shirts, sweatpants, basketball shorts, socks, sneakers, Walkman, and cassettes covers much of his living room floor. Tchaka stands in the middle of the room, frowning and scratching his brow, as if he were trying to determine who in his right mind could have made such a mess. At his feet sits an empty gym bag.

We have little time to waste. We're supposed to arrive at Kennedy Airport in just over an hour, and Tchaka's friend Steve Walston, who promised to drive us there in his van, isn't answering the phone. Tchaka inspects the pile at his feet and cautiously removes from it an item that may or may not be a bologna sandwich. All the rest he throws into his gym bag. Then he sprints toward his bedroom, pulling up short at the doorway. "Oh, God." Massive snowdrifts of dirty laundry obscure most of the floor. Tchaka spots a pair of Nikes he wants in the far corner of the room. But how to reach them? (A pair of snowshoes might help.) He blazes a trail, kicking the laundry under his bed as he goes. Then he stops in his tracks. "I forgot the loot!" he cries. "I can't go to Nike without the loot. We better get the loot. Now."

The loot, it turns out, is $60 that Annette Shipp has pledged to the Tchaka-at-Nike fund. Tchaka climbs into my two-door Toyota, folding his enormous frame into the cramped front seat like a collapsible piece of lawn furniture, and we're off, heading into downtown Jamaica to meet his mom on this first hot day of summer. "Gonna be a lot of tall guys at Nike," he says, his knees by his ears. "Lotta big, big guys." Tchaka dribbles his imaginary ball in the front seat. "Worked on my jump shot yesterday. Sometimes if I don't shoot, I forget how the ball feels." Tchaka, facing forward, looks at me out of the corner of his eye. "Got the touch back, though."

On our way into town, we drive past the playground where Tchaka often works out. A lot of puny junior high-schoolers play there, and sometimes Tchaka joins their pick-up games for the sole purpose of going on wild, uncontested dunk rampages. But yesterday he passed up the cheap thrills, keeping to himself for some last-minute preparation. "I watched games three and four of the Detroit-Lakers series last night," he tells me. "Watched Georgetown-UNLV this morning. Picked up some good moves." His face is turned in my direction now, but his eyes have gone vague. "Yup, gonna be a lot a big, big guys out there."

Annette Shipp is standing on the corner when we pull up. Like Tchaka, she is as friendly as she is tall, with an easy manner and a fondness for the privileges of motherhood, which include a mock-stern attitude toward a son who never gets into any real trouble. "I was gonna browse in the shops during lunch," she informs Tchaka as the loot changes hands, "but now I'm completely broke. I don't know why I even put my money in the bank, since you take it all. You burn a hole in my pocket, boy." She punches Tchaka on the shoulder. Tchaka, taking advantage of having a stocky, six-foot mother, socks her back. "Are you all ready, precious? Did you clean your room?" she asks. Tchaka assures her everything is in order, but Mrs. Shipp fixes him with a prosecutorial stare. "Or did you just stuff all that crap under your bed?"

For a moment, Tchaka works up a look of genuine aggrievement, but it takes too much effort in this heat. "I'll call you when I get out there," he says with a smile.

"Not collect, you won't. Now you behave yourself, okay?" She cranes upward to kiss him goodbye. "And don't go spending all that money before you leave."

Tchaka climbs back into my car. As we pull away from the curb, his mother yells after us, "Now that I'm broke, I think I'll go straight home and take a look under that bed. 'Cause if that room's a mess, I'll just call the airport and tell them to turn the plane right around! Don't you smile at me, boy — I'm *mad!*"

"She's kidding about checking under the bed," Tchaka assures me as we drive off. Then he adds, "You better step on it anyway."

I follow Tchaka's instructions, considering that we have less than forty-five minutes before we need to be at the airport. But as I slow for a red light, Tchaka snaps his fingers and gives me an imploring look. "Five minutes, okay?" And before I have come to a complete stop, he lurches from my car into Modell's Sporting Goods on Jamaica Avenue. A moment later, he's back with two pairs of spandex bike shorts in his hand and $20 less of the loot in his pocket. "If I'm gonna play with the best," he says, explaining that he plans to wear them beneath his Nike uniform, "I gotta look my best."

We're back at Tchaka's house, with less than half an hour to go, when Steve finally arrives. Actually he's still down the block, but Big Daddy Kane rapping out of his van's sound system heralds his arrival, shattering the serenity of Tchaka's street, drowning out the Mister Softee truck, and bringing one of Tchaka's neighbors inquisitively to her front door. People see Steve and his full complement of gold tooth caps and figure Tchaka must be falling in with the wrong crowd. And to tell the truth, Tchaka doesn't usually turn down one of Steve's invitations to "quit the crib" and go "questing for girls" back in Bed-Stuy, as long as he has the tranquillity of his home in Queens to return to at the end of the long night. But most evenings it's academic anyway, with Tchaka under house arrest by his mother until he finishes all his homework.

Suddenly, the door to Tracie's room swings open and Tracie emerges, looking annoyed. "What's with all the jungle bungle music?" she yells. "Steve here?" She watches as Tchaka pulls off his sweatpants and throws on a new pair of cotton basketball jams. "Oh, Tchaka, look at them — they're all wrinkled! Give them to me. I'll iron them while you finish packing."

"Nah, I like them this way — so no one knows they're new."

"Suit yourself, but you better hurry up. You've only got a half-hour."

Tchaka throws his sweats on again, grabs his bag, and is

almost out the door when he says, "Where's my *New Jack City* tape? I can't go without that tape." But he doesn't fetch it. He catches sight of himself in the living room mirror and stands there, admiring. "I'm *killin'!*"

"Tchaka, LET'S GO!" Tracie yells, dragging her brother through the doorway by his wrist.

In the street, Tchaka greets Steve but regards the van warily, as if he would ride in it to his own execution. "I can't go to Nike like this. Hold on. Better put my UNLV cap on." He runs back inside.

Steve, who has been standing proprietarily next to his van, now takes a step toward Tracie. "Does the Pretty Young Thang wanna come for a ride to the airport?"

"Yeah, I'll come along," Tracie says, backpedaling. "But how 'bout you stop calling me that?"

Steve's van is idling in the street like a Sherman tank, belching exhaust. We wait for Tchaka. We wait some more. The Shipps live right by Kennedy Airport, but this is cutting it close. Tracie checks her watch: twenty minutes and counting. Has Tchaka stolen away through his bedroom window, waiting for us to go on without him? But no, here he is with his cap and no more forgotten items, ducking with a fugitive look into the front seat of the van. Tracie and I climb in back.

A mile from Kennedy, fifteen minutes until we're due at the airport, we run into midday gridlock. Each time the van lurches to a halt, Tchaka drums his fingers impatiently on the dashboard. Finally he rolls down his window, leans out, and, making a pistol with his hand, screams at the driver stopped in front of us: "Move yo' ass or lose it!"

"Tchaka, it's a red light!" Tracie says. "What do you want him to do?" But Tchaka fixes the driver's head in his crosshairs and — *bam!* — blows it straight off. Tracie reaches over the front seat and strokes her brother's head. "Relax, Tchaka, you're gonna make your flight. And Tchaka?" She takes his head in both hands and turns it so that she can look him in the eye. "You're gonna do just fine out there."

•

Certain elements of high school basketball never seem to change, no matter where the game is played: the long wooden fold-out bleachers packed with screaming fans, cheerleaders chanting their rhythmic babble, late-afternoon sunlight slanting through the high gym windows and illuminating the yellowish columns of dust. And the singular sounds of a gym — the shouts and whistles, the squeak of sneakers, the resolute tom-tom beat of the bouncing ball that can send you in one Proustian instant right back into short pants. But the game is also changing in ways that have rendered it almost unrecognizable, now that the enormous interest generated by college basketball during the 1980s has begun to trickle down to the high school level. Gone are the yellow school buses bringing teams to the big game across town. Today the best high school teams play national schedules and Christmas tournaments in Vegas, and the top players compete in the McDonald's All-American Slam Jam game broadcast each year on ESPN. Once a team is nationally ranked — *USA Today* runs a list, the "Super 25," of the best high school programs — the players can expect complimentary sneakers from the shoe companies looking to recruit future superstars and possible TV pitchmen, while the high school coaches receive annual stipends for keeping their players shod with the proper brand.

For the most part, the money and glamour go to the parochial schools, which ensure themselves a steady talent flow by fielding several teams — varsity, junior varsity, and freshman — all coached by full-time staffs. In New York and many other cities the Catholic leagues also siphon off the best public school players by offering a safer environment, better academic preparation, and travel budgets for out-of-town tournaments. One year Saint Raymond's, a parochial school in the Bronx, took its players to Hawaii, San Diego, and Anchorage.

The Lincoln players, though they remain outside the parochial school system because of its prohibitive tuition fees and also because of Coney Island's geographical remove, get swept up by hoop hysteria as soon as the school year ends. During July and August, all the best public and parochial school players barnstorm the East Coast with the independent summer-league teams and make appearances before the college coaches and scouts at the summer camps. There, before a player's senior year, the recruiting begins in earnest while newsletters like *The Hoop Scoop* and *Big East Briefs* offer play-by-plays, venturing early predictions about where the stars may sign in the fall. "Arkansas is in tight" with one blue-chipper, *The Hoop Scoop* reports, "but the word is Indiana may be the leader." Of another player: "We understand that the mother really likes Florida State."

And the frenzy reaches its peak each summer at the Nike all-American camp. There are scores of basketball camps across the country competing for the top high school talent, but Nike is one of the only invitational, tuition-free camps. A committee of professional scouts selects 120 players — twenty-four at each position — and groups them into twelve teams, so that every game throughout the week becomes an all-star spectacle. The camp brings together players from inner-city neighborhoods in New York, Baltimore, Chicago, Detroit, Los Angeles; kids from the rural South who may never have been to a city (let alone on a plane) before; and often a small minority of white players who are the reigning spot shooters in their state but may have done most of their practicing in suburban driveways.

Tchaka earned his invitation to Nike when Bob Gibbons, a professional scout, saw him in a Virginia tournament last spring, where Tchaka played, arguably, the best ball of his young life. Nevertheless, he was selected less for his ability than for his potential — his height and his athletic build — or "the Big P," in the coaches' argot. He arrives at Nike rated 95th out of the 120 players, and his Lincoln average of 10 points per game is tied for the lowest in the camp. Ever since we left New York, Tchaka has been tormenting himself with visions of his own spectacular failure, culminating with his gloomy assessment as our plane touches down in Indianapolis: "If I don't play well this week, I'll end up at junior college in Iowa."

Most of Tchaka's competition has beaten us to the hotel by the time we arrive. The lobby of the University Place Hotel — Kiwanis country most days of the week — has been seized by an occupying army of stunningly tall black teenagers. They are lounging on the couches, lining the stairs, leaning against potted plants. On each side of the corridor connecting the lobby with a concourse of fast-food shops, players are sitting on the floor, stretching out their legs cramped from hours in flight. Each time a hotel guest approaches, casting uneasy glances at this gauntlet of dark limbs, the legs separate in synchronicity to let them by.

Tchaka scans the crowd and recognizes a dozen or so faces from New York tournament games, as well as another handful that appear to be from back home, given the signature New York look: cap turned backward, one pant leg hitched above the calf, and a punkish expression that wears well on the city's streets. But the majority are strangers whose feats on the court he has only read about in *The Hoop Scoop* and elsewhere. Talk among them is minimal. Pressing their cheeks against the heels of their hands, they watch Tchaka and the other late arrrivals through half-closed lids. When a marquee player arrives — Jason Kidd, the Oakland point guard, or Rod Rhodes, swingman from Jersey City (the nation's number-one- and two-ranked players in the summer of 1991) — I can see the apprehension ripple across the lobby, like wind over water. "This camp can make you or break you," one player whispers to his neighbor. But Tchaka doesn't catch the remark, nor recognize how evenly distributed is the anxiety in this room. Confusing the players' sullen looks for emblems of their self-confidence, Tchaka takes a seat in the corner where he can inspect the whole assemblage. It's hard to figure out who plays which position, because even the guards look like grown men, but as Tchaka feared there are a lot of big, big guys: by his count more than thirty over six feet eight, including four seven-footers. When he thinks no one is looking, he quietly drops his head into his hands.

Soon the last few campers straggle in and a Nike administrator begins to call off the players' names. One by one they walk, with loose limbs and toes turned inward, into the equipment room to claim their gear. In addition to plane fare, hotel room, and three meals a day served in a private dining hall, the campers receive free basketball uniforms, polo shirts, shorts, socks, and sneakers — all, of course, with the trademark Nike swoosh. Later on, when the players are being assigned to their teams and the administrator gets to Tchaka Shipp, he mangles the name so completely that it sounds like "Chocolate Chip." Mocking laughter arises from the entire group. Feeling the glare of a hundred pairs of competitive eyes, Tchaka raises his hand in acknowledgment — *Yes, that's me: Mr. Chocolate Chip.*

•

Many aspects of Indianapolis life — from the conspicuous absence of homeless people on the street to the suburban arrangement of diagonal parking spaces — have elicited comments from at least some members of this mostly black, mostly inner-city crowd. And the camp's athletic facilities are no exception. Nike has arranged for the games this week to be played a few blocks from the hotel at the National Institute for Fitness and Sport, a world-class training facility where the NBA's Indiana Pacers practice during the preseason. "How was your day, gentlemen?" asks an NIFS staff member, opening the door for the players on their first afternoon of competition. Stunned by the lavish surroundings, the players exchange looks and descend in virtual silence through several tiers of chrome and plate glass to a changing room with plush carpeting and polished wood lockers, each accessible by a specially coded magnetic card. Nearby, reporters from across the country have begun to collect around the media clearance center to pick up the latest rosters of the players and to bet among themselves which highly rated stars will embarrass themselves this week and which dark horses may thrive.

I'm standing outside the locker room, talking to a camp administrator and a few of Tchaka's teammates, when Tchaka appears in his underwear, holding his uniform in his hand. "Coach. My locker closed on me," he says helplessly. "You gotta let me in again." Tchaka's teammates sigh while Tchaka follows the administrator back into the locker room. Several minutes pass. In the arena next door we can hear a booming voice over the public address system calling players by name to the court where their games are scheduled. Still no sign of Tchaka. Finally, I am dispatched to find him, and I come upon Tchaka peering over his shoulder at his reflection in the locker room mirror, checking to see whether his new bike shorts are sufficiently visible beneath his uniform. He slaps my hand and says, "I'm the man." Then we rejoin his team and walk down the narrow corridor toward the main arena.

Most interior spaces are drawn more or less to the same human scale, so when I walk through the arena doors I think at first that I am staring at one basketball court reflected in a series of mirrors, like tables in a small restaurant. But when my eyes adjust to the space, I realize that under this domed roof, vast enough to cover a three-ring circus, Nike officials have arranged for three professional-length courts, ninety-four feet each, installed side by side. Metal grandstands for the college coaches rise behind each court. On the sidelines are team benches, scorers' tables, water coolers, first-aid stations, and the ubiquitous Nike banners. Circling it all is a quarter-mile track. On the waxy, blond-wood courts themselves are NBA-style baskets; their rims snap back after a player dunks, and they are attached to backboards mounted on hydraulic bases. Most of the teams have already formed lay-up lines, and Tchaka, getting his foot taped by a trainer at the sidelines, watches as each of the players — six-eight, six-nine, six-nine, six-*eleven* — flies toward the basket, delivering the full menu of dunks: double-pumps, tomahawks, windmills, reverses, 360s. One kid jumps so high he dunks at chest level, causing Tchaka to take in breath involuntarily. From all six baskets come the sounds of jamming — the fearsome ka-*thunk* of fiberglass and steel undergoing grueling and repeated punishment.

Soon a low but persistent hum, like the sound of tires on a freeway, fills the arena: the college coaches are starting to filter in, chatting with one another; and the players are spying on the coaches, whispering among themselves. Within a few minutes, Tchaka has spotted Duke's Mike Krzyzewski, Indiana's Bobby Knight, Georgetown's John Thompson, Seton Hall's P. J. Carlesimo, Villanova's Rollie Massimino, as well as a legion of lesser known coaches, most of them with the obligatory uniform: mustache, V-neck sweater, and clipboard poised on polyester knee. Only twice a year do so many top Division I coaches congregate in the same arena: the Nike all-American camp and the Final Four tournament. Later in the summer, the coaching staffs — a head coach and up to three assistants at the bigger schools — will split

up to cover as many camps as possible. But it would consti-
tute professional malpractice for them not to show up in
unison at Nike today. This, after all, is the official beginning
of the NCAA's summer evaluation period, the finest high
school players in the country are about to go head to head,
and future NCAA titles may well hinge on which coach
watches the competition this week with the most discrimi-
nating eye.

Yesterday, in a practice scrimmage before the arrival of
the coaches, Tchaka got his first chance to test the mettle
of his competition. Eager to establish himself, as soon as his
coach sent him in he began jostling for position against the
player guarding him — a lot of intense, meaningless activity, as it turned out, since the kid, a seven-foot sequoia,
summarily dismissed Tchaka from the low post with a single forearm shove. On his second trip downcourt, Tchaka,
in the confusion of battle, attempted to block a shot by
his own teammate — then quickly pulled his hand away,
as though he had touched something hot. Happily, no one
but his irked teammate seemed to notice. From now on,
however, all mistakes go directly into the record book. As
Tchaka warms up for his first official game, I can see John
McLeod, the head coach at Notre Dame, lean over to his
assistant. "Look at the body on that kid! Where's he from?"
McLeod admires Tchaka's physique until Tchaka misses a
few practice shots. "He's got no outside shot," the coach
says, sounding personally betrayed. Tchaka sends another
fifteen-footer clanging off the front rim. "Man, he's got no
outside shot at all.". Shaking his head, McLeod turns his
attention to other players.

Games on all three courts will begin at just about the
same time, and the arena grows still with expectation as the
refs walk to center court. As soon as the ball goes up, the
play is fast and ferociously athletic — a back-and-forth game
with no team wasting much of its shot clock. It quickly

becomes evident who will dominate during this week of unstructured, run-and-gun ball: the point guards, who are controlling the dribble and often launch three-pointers before making a single pass, and the true Goliaths, six-ten and up, who linger beneath the basket with a claim on anything that doesn't fall cleanly through the hoop. Tchaka, when he is sent into the game, seems caught in the middle. He lacks the skill to put the ball on the floor and maneuver a path to the basket, and he doesn't have the confidence yet to shoot from the perimeter. So his teammates aren't giving him the ball, and when he does come into possession, the pressure to seize the moment seems to have numbed his better instincts. Instead of shooting quickly or making the smart pass, he simply holds the ball or dribbles in place — either of which brings the opposing guards swooping down in a double team to strip him of the ball. Losing possession, Tchaka is beside himself with agitation, looking to the ref for a foul call and muttering, "Shit! Shit!" while the rest of his team sprints to the opposite end of the floor. The next trip downcourt, determined not to hesitate, he makes his move to the basket before he's got the ball in his grip and drops it into enemy hands. "Damn! Damn!" This could easily turn out to be a painful week of play for Tchaka, and if that is the case, not a lot of fun to watch either.

But then, in his final minute of play, Tchaka slips out of his self-consciousness and suddenly he is playing as he does in his mind's eye — stifling his man on defense, deflecting the pass. He's forced the turnover! Now his point guard picks up the ball, and it's fast-break time — Tchaka and his teammates are all sprinting downcourt with wild looks in their eyes. Tchaka claims the right lane, his favorite spot, and he's crossing the open terrain with leaping gazelle strides. He calls for the pass and gets it. Yes! Now there's no one — can this be true? — standing between Tchaka and the basket. It's almost time for take-off. Two dribbles and he leans hard on the throttle, and now he's airborne! Here's sweet redemption — the orange rim zooming toward his eyeballs. Spontaneous regression to a preverbal state: "*Aaaargh!*" He's still up there, spiraling from the rim like a mobile as the buzzer sounds, and I'm on my feet, cheering amid a sea of stone-faced coaches busily scratching notes about the players in their programs.

On balance, it seems to me, Tchaka has acquitted himself fairly well on this, his first day of competition. And, with small variations, this is how he continues to play during these early games — making some mistakes, then showing flashes of his potential. But when I join him on the sidelines after his third outing, he refuses even to look at me. While his team huddles, he sits on the bench, balling and unballing his fists. Amid the postgame flurry of lockers banging open and shut, players' voices echoing off the tile shower walls, and the sound of rolled-up towels making contact with bare skin — *thwack!* — Tchaka dresses in silence. He walks back to the hotel alone, cursing himself like a lunatic while his shorts ride lower and lower on his hips. Things go on like this until dinnertime, at which point Tchaka selects an empty table and spends most of the meal methodically picking the *a la king* off his chicken, then leaving the whole glutinous mess uneaten on his plate. Laughter from other precincts drifts over, and eventually Tchaka's table begins to fill with some kids who seem to have enjoyed a better start to their week of camp. Tchaka won't look up, even as a spirited discussion commences all around him:

— Here's my secret: you got to be a ball hog at this camp. 'Cause if you ain't, somebody else is.

— Man, as soon as them niggers *touch* the ball, they're pullin'.

— You hoopin'? I'm hoopin' next game, shooting every time I touch the ball.

— I eat this apple pie? Guaranteed to hit my threes. You eat your pie? Guaranteed to dunk.

— Who's that nigger dunked from the foul line wearing L.A. Gear?

— I saw that. He *threw* it on him.

— You get dunked on yet?

— Not in public!

— Everybody gonna get dunked on at some point this week.

— It's part of the game.

— Yeah, that's just a fact of life.

"Not me," Tchaka growls. "No one's gonna dunk on me." All eyes turn toward him. But Tchaka has nothing more he wants to share with the group. Moments later he picks up his tray and walks away.

•

Officially, the Nike camp is known as the ABCD program. The acronym stands for Academic Betterment and Career Development, and the players must take math and English classes from nine to twelve each morning and attend a lunchtime lecture by a guest speaker before the games begin in the afternoon. Speaking in the auditorium of the University Place Hotel, Frank Dubois, a Nike administrator, explains during the first of the daily lectures, "We don't like to call this a camp. It's an *academic program* to get you guys ready for college." In the world of high school basketball — in which the concept of the student-athlete often seems to rely primarily on its hyphen — such distinctions are crucial. Although every camper here has the potential to play at one of the nation's top college programs, if past statistics are any guide most of them will arrive at school with no idea how to take lecture notes, read a college text, use a library, or write a research paper. Scrambling from the start of freshman year to keep pace with their classmates, the players will then be called upon to spend an average of twenty hours a week in practice, another fifteen traveling to games. Fewer than half of them will graduate in even five years.

This particular group of Nike athletes looks to be in similar peril. Early in the week, all the players were tested on math and reading comprehension. A few days later, the results were in. "Are there any TV cameras in here?" asks a Nike staffer. "No? Good." Then he announces that of the 120 campers, twenty-three read at the ninth-grade level or above; some read at the third-grade level. (Tchaka tested reasonably well, but he clowned around enough so that his peers would never suspect.) The daily lectures are given over to cautionary tales, like the one about a twenty-two-year-old college star who ignored his academic problems until, ordering dinner at a restaurant for himself and his girlfriend, it was discovered that he couldn't read the menu. The players are asked, "Your bachelor of athletics will be over by the time you're twenty-one. Then what will you do?" And: "Do you think God put you on this earth just to play basketball?"

Academic discipline is presented as the sensible alternative to the delusions of celebrity, wealth, and stardom in the NBA. Nike instructors offer practical lessons in concentration, note taking, time management, and the most effective way to take multiple choice tests. In some ways, the players receive better teaching and more individual attention than most of them have ever seen in high school. Some players couldn't care less, trading tips on the best way to sleep in class with their eyes open. Midway through the week, one teacher leaves the room for a drink of water and his class uses its newly acquired time-management skills to move the clock ahead twenty minutes. Among other kids, however, a quiet transformation takes place. One tough New York kid with whom Tchaka has become friendly (he of the hitched pant leg and sour expression) has relaxed within days of leaving the city. Here at Nike he is meeting lots of thoughtful, sweet-tempered kids who can also wreak havoc on the court, which forces him to question long-held assumptions linking basketball prowess with thuggery. By midweek Tchaka's friend is carrying his teacher's bag to class and has written an essay about how in New York he sometimes sneaks into his high school library so that his friends won't see. (Toward the end of the week, unhappily, he receives the news that one of his best friends has been shot and killed on a Brooklyn street. The process goes into reverse: the pant leg is rehitched, the cap turns backward, and by the time he lands at Kennedy he is stealing doughnuts from airport vendors.)

But despite the attention to academics and all the talk among the Nike staff of "doing what's right for the kids," a certain cognitive dissonance becomes apparent to many of the players. If this is a fresh-air camp for disadvantaged inner-city youth, why are there so many solemn-faced coaches, scouting services, *Hoop Scoop* reporters, and ESPN camera crews recording their every move? And if playing professional ball is a pipe dream, why, one kid wonders aloud, was that guest speaker from Nike just introduced to the players as "the man you can sign your endorsement contract with when you make it to the NBA"?

From the time the campers first arrived, they have been told, on an almost hourly basis, to concentrate on the academics and, as for the basketball, "just go out there and have fun." But the measure of these kids' athletic ability is being taken constantly, all week and in dozens of different ways. As the competition progresses, the media center churns out daily stat sheets that break down every element of the kids' play. (Like the NBA all-star game, no one cares who wins or loses; the college coaches can't even see the scoreboard from where they sit.) In addition to precise measurements of height, weight, and body fat, every player is put through a battery of tests to gauge his quickness on the forty-yard dash, vertical reach, hang time, arm span, and strength of grip. (The camp swears the information is kept confidential, but who knows?) The official Nike roster, produced for the benefit of the visiting coaches, includes the Nike selection committee's appraisal, often minutely observed. A forward from the Bronx possesses "the best first step of any player." A small forward from Florida has a "velvety, accurate shooting touch to 22 feet." Frankness outweighs diplomacy: a Florida forward, according to the roster, "needs to lose 15–20 pounds to improve his stamina." A seven-foot junior "appears to lack motivation," in the estimation of the Nike shoe company. "His coach proclaims him the best big man ever in Chicago. We have our doubts." For his part, Tchaka is called a "budding young power player" and "a warrior on the block." Given the general whiteness of the coaches and the overwhelming blackness of the players, whose every physical attribute is being scrutinized, certain analogies are inevitably drawn. The one that appears as a headline this week in the *Indianapolis News* is among the more charitable: CAMP RESEMBLES STATE FAIR CATTLE EXHIBITION.

•

By midweek, Tchaka is beginning to hit his stride. Realizing his teammates are never going to run a set play for him, he is finding other ways to get the ball in his hands: blocking shots, boxing out for rebounds, fearlessly hurling himself to the floor for loose balls. Whenever a teammate misses on a fast break, Tchaka is right there with a put-back. He still makes mistakes that set his teammates' eyeballs rolling, like playfully slapping his point guard's ass as he dribbles, knocking the ball into an opponent's hands. But they are mistakes now of enthusiasm rather than of tentativeness. And his play in the open court gives him enough confidence that when he does get the ball in the half-court offense, he no longer flails or hesitates — he locates his defender, then passes or shoots with dispatch and a surprising new confidence to his moves. "Watch the pick!" he yells to his teammates on defense, and calls out, "My fault, my fault," whenever his own man gets by him for a basket. Tchaka still wishes he were playing a more freewheeling game — executing spin moves and turnaround jumpers like those he sees all around him. Except for his dunks, his moments with the ball come without much glamour or instant gratification. But he's beginning to stand out for the coaches, who comment on his quickness, his enthusiasm, and the little things — his defensive rotations and outlet passes — that reveal how well Coach Hartstein has taught him the game.

And Tchaka's mood, though it still lags behind his performance, is gradually improving. On the third day, while two new teams take the court, Tchaka sits in the bleachers with his teammate Lawrence Thomas. They pore over their stats, watch the game intermittently, and indulge in the guarded, laconic talk of two strangers suddenly bound together in the same scary but exciting new enterprise.

"How many dunks you got today?" asks Lawrence.

"Three," Tchaka replies. "How many three-pointers you got?"

"Three."

They look up in tandem. On the court, a player drives baseline from right to left and floats up a gorgeous reverse lay-up. A small riot of appreciative hooting erupts among the sidelined players. The coaches remain silent as always, but you can see their heads dropping to locate the shooter's name on the rosters in their laps: "Dontonio Wingfield . . . 6–8 . . . 235 lbs. . . . tremendous physical specimen."

"You got your confidence?" asks Lawrence.

"I still feel a little jittery," Tchaka replies, "but, yeah, got mine today. You got yours?"

"Yeah."

At the other end of the court, a lithe forward slashes through midlane traffic and lifts a scoop shot over the outstretched hand of his defender. ("Donta Bright . . . 6–6 . . . 190 lbs. . . . built like a greyhound.")

"You the man now," Lawrence says to Tchaka.

"You my little point guard," Tchaka replies, patting Lawrence's head.

"We got ourselves a relationship," Lawrence observes.

"Partners," Tchaka agrees.

They shake hands.

"'Cause we so far away from home."

•

"Yup, a lotta horses here," remarked Tom Sullivan, one of Seton Hall's assistant coaches, on the first day of camp. Now he and his boss, the Pirates' head coach, P. J. Carlesimo, take seats in the first row of grandstands to watch one of Tchaka's games. The week is two-thirds over and Tchaka is playing harder and more intensely than I have ever seen. On a fast break, he trails his new buddy, Lawrence. Lawrence misses the shot, which caroms back toward Tchaka. Tchaka skies for the ball and jams it back in, only to be undercut by another player as he dangles from the rim. Felled like a tree, Tchaka crashes to the floor with a seismic *thump*, but he bounds back to his feet, smiling and shaking his poor cudgeled wits and trotting downcourt for more.

Carlesimo and Sullivan exchange admiring, arched-eyebrow looks. Every time they watch one of Tchaka's games, they glance behind them to see who else may be watching. One day it was Providence coach Rick Barnes and his assistant Fran Fraschilla sitting at one end of the bleachers. (Carlesimo waved to Barnes, then turned back toward the game with a slight grimace.) Today it's Rollie Massimino of Villanova, up there watching with his assistant. ("Hey, Rollie, what's up?")

With top college conferences like the Big East earning as much as $65 million for a one-year contract with CBS Sports, the pressure on coaches like Carlesimo, Barnes, and Massimino to recruit the top stars at Nike is not significantly less than it is for the players themselves: jobs and livelihoods are on the line for the coaches; success in the NCAA tournament and million-dollar TV contracts are on the line for their schools. Given the intense competition among the recruiters here at Nike, and the widespread suspicion that not all of them follow religiously the NCAA rules governing the recruiting process, it isn't surprising that collegiality among the coaches often suffers serious injury. At one point, a small-time Division II coach walks toward the Seton Hall duo, then stops and points at Carlesimo's handbag. "Whaddaya got there?" he asks with a smile.

"Money," Carlesimo replies acidly. "I'm going recruiting." The DII scurries away.

A few rows behind the Seton Hall staff, Bobby Knight takes a seat next to the TV commentator Dick Vitale, and the two can be heard discussing how shocked, *shocked* they were to discover that one Big East coach has apparently been offering stereos to recruits.

Just to their right, a man hoists a video camera onto his shoulder. I watch for a few minutes as he rakes it back and forth across the court, simultaneously dictating a play-by-play into the camera's mike. Then I realize the equipment is trained on Tchaka. Not recognizing the man, and wondering whether he is a street agent or an "alumni rep," commonly employed by colleges to bypass NCAA rules governing the conduct of coaches, I introduce myself. He lowers his camera and offers a glacial stare until I back away.

Among the NCAA's myriad rules regulating the recruiting process is one that allows college coaches to watch — but not speak to — any player during the summer camp season. Last year, when the Nike camp was held in a cramped arena in Princeton, New Jersey, players walking on and off the court were instructed to look the other way so that coaches could not make eye contact with them. Here in Indianapolis, the players have to sit on a bleacher separated from the coaches by yellow police tape. Nevertheless, the coaches have developed ingenious strategies for advertising their presence to the players. The well-known faces — Bobby Knight, John Thompson, Kentucky's Rick Pitino — simply sit midbleacher and wait for the players to spot them. The less recognizable coaches wear T-shirts with giant school logos and stand up to stretch on a regular basis. Carlesimo and Sullivan have begun sitting just three feet behind Tchaka's bench. Carlesimo rarely acknowledges me, but Sullivan always chats pleasantly for a minute, then says, "Tell Tchaka we were watching."

If a coach and a recruit do come into "unavoidable" contact, according to Rule 13.1.2.3–(e) of the NCAA manual, the two may exchange "normal civility." Certain coaches give this clause a fairly broad interpretation. Fran Fraschilla of Providence, for example, lingers in public areas — hotels, airport lounges — looking to (as the coaches like to say) "get some bump," a chance encounter that may allow for an "unavoidable" exchange of pleasantries. A week after the Nike camp, Tchaka was walking down the hall at another basketball camp, complaining to his roommate about the dorm rooms they had been assigned. There was the unavoidable Fraschilla. "How ya doin'?" he asked.

"All right," Tchaka replied, "but they got us in a real dump."

"Oh, yeah? I'm staying at the Holiday Inn. It's nice."

Fraschilla laughed nervously, perhaps wondering whether he was going too far. "I got the A.C. turned up, and we got a pool, too."

"Got some girls?" asked Tchaka's roommate.

"Well, I just called my wife, but I might be able to fix *you* guys up." The coach laughed again, then seemed to think better of the whole encounter and backpedaled away from the two players, still laughing, a hand extended by way of apology.

Throughout the week at Nike, camp administrators advise the players on how to stay out of trouble with the recruiters and scouts who attend the camp at the company's invitation. One day Edward McDonald, a former assistant U.S. Attorney who prosecuted several Boston College players for a point-shaving conspiracy in the late 1970s, drops by to give a lunchtime lecture. "Watch out for guys who want to get close to you," he instructs. "Also, if someone takes you to dinner and makes an illegal offer, you've got to get up and leave the table *before* you take something — either money or a free meal . . ." Even an innocent association with a disreputable character, the players are warned, could ruin their careers. Witness Anderson Hunt, the only UNLV starter last year not to get drafted, primarily because of published photographs showing him in a Jacuzzi with the reputed gambler Richard (the Fixer) Perry.

"Basketball players have celebrity status," another guest speaker tells the players. "There are going to be women in your face" — much cheering from the campers — "oh, yeah, women, charlatans, agents who want an association with you and want a fast buck. You'll be offered money, cars, and even female students when you're being recruited." Another outburst from the audience, and Nike staffers move in from the sides to quiet the group down. "But if you're caught, I'm telling you: your career is finished." At the Nike camp, the players are warned not to use the restroom at the sports arena because one never knows who might suddenly come out from behind a stall or sidle up to them at an adjacent urinal. "Oh, and one last thing," the players are told as the meeting breaks up. "Don't make any calls from the arena's pay phone either. The college coaches hang around there too. All you need before your senior season is to be seen around a coach. Another college coach who wants to recruit you doesn't like it, calls the NCAA, and you'll both get investigated. All right, time to get changed into your uniforms. Games begin in half an hour. Now just go out there and have fun."

•

From time to time this week, I look into the stands and spot a heavyset man with narrow eyes and dark hair in middle-aged retreat. He always wears a pastel Nike sports shirt and a sated look, as though he's been feasting his eyes on the proceedings and has just now got his fill. Each time I glance at him, a college coach, a high school player, a high school coach, or a reporter is standing one bleacher step below him, paying his respects. The man receives his visitors without taking his eyes off the court. Then he offers his hand a second time, indicating that the visitor consider taking his leave. One day I ask Tchaka who he is, and Tchaka informs me, "That's Sonny Vaccaro, you idiot. He the man!"

I should have known. If it weren't for Vaccaro, none of us would be here in Indianapolis — nor, most likely, would Nike be the pre-eminent sneaker company in the United States today, with more than $400 million in sales of basketball shoes and apparel alone. Vaccaro has done more to influence basketball than just about anyone who doesn't actually play the game. While other sneaker companies have gone the traditional route, simply advertising their wares, Vaccaro discovered a brand-new way to penetrate the sneaker market. With Nike's multimillion-dollar sports marketing bud-

get, he began signing up almost a hundred of college basketball's top coaches, including Seton Hall's P. J. Carlesimo,
Georgetown's John Thompson, Syracuse's Jim Boeheim, and
Duke's Mike Krzyzewski, to exclusive six-figure endorsement
contracts. (To lure Krzyzewski away from Adidas, Nike paid
him a million-dollar signing bonus, plus $375,000 a year.) Os-
tensibly, the coaches are paid to offer product advice. But Nike
is less interested in discovering what the coaches may think
of their new cushioned sole than in encouraging them to keep
Nike sneakers on the most talented and visible feet in the
business — the college stars who influence schoolyard fashion
and may also graduate to become the next great Nike endorsers: the David Robinsons, Charles Barkleys, and Michael Jordans of the future.

The ABCD camp is an extension of this marketing strategy. It costs the company an estimated $200,000 to stage the
camp each year. But it's an investment, allowing the long
arms of Nike to reach ever deeper into the heart of the
game, bringing the best high school players into the Nike
fold. Many of the 120 players here this week have a long and
intimate relationship with Nike, whether they know it or
not. At Lincoln, for example, Tchaka receives his sneakers
from Nike. Tchaka's association with his summer team, the
Madison Square Boys Club, also earns him a pair of free
Nikes. There are probably another two hundred kids in the
country with Tchaka's potential, but he is here this week,
not they, in part because he comes from a Nike high school
program, plays with a Nike summer-league team, and has
conveyed some interest in going to a Nike college (Syracuse
and Seton Hall). Shoe company officials insist that Nike
has no influence over where its campers eventually sign,
and they bridle at the suggestion that the camp may be
construed as a farm league for Nike prospects. But even as
camp officials are lecturing players on how to avoid exploi-

tative college recruiters, Nike is bestowing on its campers an astonishing largess — sneakers, shirts, shorts, meals, airfare, hotel room — that would be considered a blatantly illegal inducement if it came from a college coach. But, no matter. As the commentator Dick Vitale put it in a speech to the campers this week, assuming that the way to a player's heart is through his feet, "Remember: Nike's good to you, you're good to Nike, and that's what American entrepreneurship is all about." (Vitale himself is on the Nike payroll.)

By week's end, some of the players are beginning to fit the pieces together. On the camp's final day Tchaka and I sit down for lunch at a table just as another player holds forth to his colleagues. "Sure they put us up in this plush hotel," he says, "and they give us $120 sneakers, but that's nothing." The player lowers his voice, and the other campers lean forward. "Ever wonder why you see Billy Owens's father here this week? He's Sonny's money man. And what sneakers you think Billy's gonna wear when he leaves Syracuse and plays next year in the NBA? And how much money you think Nike's gonna make from *that*?" The players exchange looks. "That's right. Nike makes plenty of money off of us, just like the colleges. Look at Patrick Ewing. He put Georgetown on the map. You hear about Georgetown before that? They made $30 million during his four years. They gave him a $15,000 scholarship — maybe $20,000 — but that's an $80,000 investment on a $30 million return." No one even lifts a fork. "Nike's got the same strategy. A hundred and twenty dollar sneakers and we're theirs for life. We *are* the game, and we gotta know our business . . ." And suddenly the dam bursts and all these kids — most of them poor, some of them just a few years away from their first million — begin talking, comparing notes, trading anecdotes about guys they knew in high school who arrived at college with rusted-out cars and were soon driving black Corvettes, and other friends who were "taken care of" in subtler ways.

For his part, Tchaka listens more than he speaks. Talking about the business end of this game always makes him nervous. "Besides," he says, "my theory is, you start to worry about all of that stuff and then you do something to impress all the coaches. That's when you really embarrass yourself and you *know* they're scratching your name off their list."

All week Tchaka has been putting his theory to the test, methodically assembling his game, piece by piece, until, by the time we walk toward our gate at Indianapolis airport for the return flight to New York, he can look at the other players sprawled around the waiting area (no longer misreading their sullen looks) and say, with a big grin, "You know, I think I can play with these guys."

With that statement Tchaka officially becomes the last person in the entire camp to realize this. Everyone else has been witnessing one of the great underdog stories of the summer season. Throughout the week, coaches at almost all the Big East schools told me they were ready to offer Tchaka scholarships then and there. *The Hoop Scoop* was calling him over to the sidelines to tell him that he was now one of the nation's premier players and to ask him where he was thinking of signing. When Tchaka went over to pay his respects to Sonny Vaccaro, also inquiring politely why his summer team hadn't received its Nikes, Vaccaro didn't look at him, but he did promise to find out what was causing the delay. (Tchaka had his new kicks by the start of the school year.)

But having hit the big time, Tchaka will not be left alone, not from now until the day in November when he chooses his school. For the rest of the summer, coaches will follow Tchaka everywhere, going to his games and practices and living in Holiday Inns up and down the East Coast to display their devotion to him; and calling Bobby Hartstein so frequently that the high school coach — whose interest in telecommunications is so scant that he prides himself on not knowing how much it costs to call Manhattan from a Brooklyn pay phone — will go out and buy an answering machine to screen his calls. Toward the end of the summer, Tchaka will even receive a series of anonymous telephone calls telling him to sign with a Nike college.

When Tchaka first arrived in Indianapolis at the beginning of the week, walking off the airplane with his six-seven frame and Michelangelo muscles, a stranger strode purposefully in his direction and, standing at least a foot below him, reached up and shook his hand. The man seemed pleased to have made Tchaka's acquaintance; he looked like a man who brings his son to the casino just for the fun of it and discovers the kid can count cards. His face was alive to possibility. He handed Tchaka his telephone number on a slip of paper. Tchaka stared at it without understanding what possible use he could make of it. "Maybe you can use me someday," the man said, with something more than charitable feeling. "If you do, now you know: I'm the man to call." By the end of the week, Tchaka had established himself as someone who would get a lot more telephone numbers and offers to be of service, usually of an unspecified nature. Tchaka would simply file them away in a shoebox in his bedroom and play by all the rules. But after his week at the Nike camp he would no longer have the slightest doubt about what they meant.

Three

IN ALMOST ALL sporting events, a moment arises in which the physical prowess of the athlete — that magical, princely quality for which he is adored — is suddenly rendered useless, for the great challenge he faces is a purely mental one. That's when things start to get interesting. Does the pitcher, hoping to prevent the base runner from stealing second, hurl his fastball, though the batter may connect? Or does he try to whiff the batter with a curve, though the runner may advance? Can the golfer properly calculate the slope of the green to sink the twelve-foot putt? In hockey . . . well, forget hockey. But basketball — now there's a sport with a fine moment of psychological suspense. Basketball, of course, has the foul shot.

What could be easier than this — the old two-handed set shot, executed with no one guarding you, while you take all the time you need? Foul shots are also called, for self-evident reasons, "free throws"; the foul line is sometimes referred to, for poetic purposes, as "the charity stripe." The most consistent NBA players make their foul shots 90 percent of the time. I have heard of high school coaches who demand that their players hit a hundred of them each day in practice, wearing a blindfold.

On the other hand, a foul shot is the one moment in this most fluid and communal of games that occurs in sheer isolation, and isolation often causes strange things to happen. Imagine. With a shrill blast of the whistle, the frenetic back-and-forth of the game abruptly ceases and the ref awards you two shots, though the spread of stomach acid you will soon feel hardly makes it seem like a gift. It is possible to get nervous shooting foul shots in an empty gym (I know), and this is not an empty gym. Beneath the basket the other players crowd for position into two rebound lines, their very presence an affront, their eager elbowing a sign of their confidence that you will miss at least the second shot. Directly behind the basket a hostile group of fans rise to their feet, screaming and waving their arms and hoping in this manner to distract you from your focus on the rim fifteen feet away. During basketball's busier moments — when you take an elbow in the ear while contesting a rebound, say, or run backward into a moving pick — the game encourages a certain forgetfulness of the crowd. Not now. Now you feel as if the gym has been plunged into darkness and a brilliant column of light illuminates your every awkward move as you step to the line, alone.

At the present moment, Russell Thomas steps to the line in the Albany High School gym in upstate New York, and waits there for the official to toss him the ball. Because this is one of the Empire State Games — a four-day tournament bringing together the finest high school players from across New York State — two bleachers filled with excitable fans rise steeply on each side of the court. The Empires, held two weeks after the Nike all-American camp, also lure a portion of the traveling crew of college coaches, here to appraise the players, who are divided this weekend into teams from New York City, Long Island, Central New York, the Adirondack region, and Western New York State. Tchaka, who joins Russell on the New York City squad, could miss all his foul shots and drop all his passes during this tournament and, after his performance in Indianapolis, still have his pick of top colleges. But this is Russell's principal stop on the summer circuit, his best chance to show the coaches what he can do with a basketball.

And as if the fans and coaches didn't increase the pressure on him, Russell has to contend also with the scoreboard, which, above him and to the right, presents a variety of information that could raise the hair on the back of his neck, if he had any. Under HOME, it indicates that the Western team now has 87 points. Under VISITORS (New York players are treated as an invasionary force wherever they go), it reveals that Russell's team has 86. Other pertinent data include the quarter we are in: fourth. And the time remaining: seven tenths of a second, which is not enough time to complete nearly any task outside the field of particle physics but is — ah, the many pleasures of this sport! — plenty of time for Russell, singlehandedly, to win or lose this game.

Now the ref tosses Russell the ball. Russell spreads his feet two-and-a-half feet apart (as he has been taught), bounces the ball five times (as is his habit), and stares at his toes. As Russell takes a deep breath and gathers himself for the shot, Tchaka suddenly leaves the rebound line, walks over to him, and whispers in his ear. "Just take it easy and don't forget to follow through," Tchaka may be saying. Or, "Don't fuck up." It's impossible to know for sure. Tchaka rubs Russell's bald head and reclaims his spot in line. Russell resets his feet, bounces the ball five additional times, and gradually lifts his head until he is staring directly at the rim. His face carries absolutely no expression.

In the stands the crowd turns up the volume on its show. The college coaches, who sit together in the first five rows, lean forward like basketball fans, which by and large they are not. Trekking from tournament to tournament all summer can be jading work; and besides, the matter of which team actually triumphs in the end, of ultimate importance to Russell and the other players at this moment, holds little interest for the recruiters, who are in the business of scouting individual talent. But this game has been restorative. The tournament's championship game, which will result in a gold medal for one of the five teams, takes place on Sunday. Since many of the coaches will be gone by then, off to the next stop on the recruiting circuit, Russell, Tchaka, and the other players have performed this afternoon with a ferocity befitting the gold-medal round. Both New York City and Western have played tenacious defense, unheard of during the summer season, and this has slowed the game and tested both teams' ability to run intelligent, half-court offenses. Grudgingly, like old men stirred from their afternoon nap, the coaches have awakened to the pleasures of watching this game.

And these crucial foul shots may prove relevant to their work after all. If scouting involved merely the estimation of physical ability, the task could be accomplished by a statistician. To predict how a high school kid will play on the highly competitive college level requires (as the coaches like to point out) an astute judgment of character. One day at the Nike camp I overheard two coaches discussing a player, a white kid from an affluent suburb. They concluded that he was "not hungry enough" to compete in college against black players from the ghetto. On another occasion I listened to a coach enumerating the various tragedies that had befallen a kid — orphaned at a young age, living in a foster home, searching endlessly for authority figures. "Bet he's *extremely* coachable," the recruiter said with enthusiasm.

In Albany for the last two days, Russell has played superbly, and the physical elements of his game — his shooting touch, his reflexes on defense — have won him many admirers in the stands. Now the talk among the coaches veers toward the psychological — whether Russell has the mental steadiness required to make the big plays. As Russell spins the ball lightly in his hands, the head coach of a mid-level Division I school leans toward his assistant. "So what's your prediction?" he says with a playful look. "Does he make these two or does he choke?"

Russell raises the ball. "This kid?" says the assistant, considering the question, savoring it, as if there were as much riding on his answer as there is right now for Russell. "From what I hear? This kid definitely chokes."

•

I had enjoyed watching Russell in his solitary workouts at the Garden last spring, but I didn't get to know him well until the final weeks of his junior year, when he and I, usually after his last class, would run errands around Coney Island in my car. Russell's father had moved away from home when Russell was young, and much of the business of taking care of his mother and his two younger sisters has fallen to him. Something of a loner, quiet in groups, Russell would turn surprisingly garrulous in my car, and what he talked about most often was his future. "Maybe I might make the NBA like Tchaka," he said to me once as we drove to a check-cashing joint a few blocks from Lincoln so that he could pay the family's telephone bill before their service was cut off. "But to be honest with you, I'm using basketball to go to a four-year school. What I really want is to graduate from college, start me a nice little family, and get me a nice little job as a registered nurse. But first I got to make sure I get that degree." We were driving beneath the elevated train tracks over Stillwell Avenue, where four of New York's subway lines come to an end just blocks from the boardwalk. Russell stared out the window at a group of young men standing around in front of a corner bodega, then raked his hand over his bald head, a gesture that often accompanies his absorption in thought. "See, where I live it's real bad. A lot of drugs, a lot of gun fights. I look at my friends.

They were going along okay, but something messed them up. I don't know." He fell silent and looked upward at the afternoon sun, strobing on and off through the slats of the train tracks, and added quietly, "I don't want to be like my friends. I want to live a nice life. They're my age, but they're already living on memories."

During those afterschool rides, I was always surprised to hear such solemn, thoughtful words coming from a kid who everyone had warned me could be such trouble. Russell, after all, had made the sports sections of several New York tabloids last year not only for averaging 19.5 points per game as a junior and leading the Lincoln team to the city championships at Madison Square Garden, but also for climbing to the top of that building in Coney Island and threatening to jump off. And he often confounded his coach and his teammates with his mysterious behavior — sneaking out of locker rooms and boycotting team dinners, often without a word of explanation. Yet in other ways Russell was the most driven and committed kid on the team. No other player in Coney Island ran wind sprints up his project stairwell or showed up at the Garden to shoot one-handers from a chair. No other kid on the Lincoln varsity spent his Saturday nights alone at his kitchen table, studying feverishly for his SATs. At eighteen, Russell seemed both younger and older than his years, which, given his upbringing, was probably inevitable.

Russell has never lived anywhere but Coney Island, and for much of his adolescence he seemed to be following on the heels of his older friends — kids who are now in gangs or prison or are just hanging out on street corners looking for something to do. But then organized basketball became the focus and obsession of his life. One day when Russell was fourteen, an assistant coach from Lincoln spotted him playing ball at the Garden and persuaded him to enroll. On the Lincoln varsity, Russell gained confidence in his game and, more important, listened closely to Coach Hartstein's inspirational speeches about where basketball might one day lead him. In class, though he suffered from years of bad teaching in grammar school and junior high, his hard work slowly began to yield results. For the first time in his life, he allowed himself to consider the possibility that he might even be bright. "I used to think there were smart people and dumb people," he said to me one day after school. "But that's not true. Everybody's got the same brain. They say a human mind can know a thousand words — it's like a little computer. But you got to practice. That's how your mind starts to expand and mature." The idea that he might enjoy a future different from that of his friends — might leave Coney Island and attend college on a basketball scholarship — began to take shape in Russell's imagination.

And then came the fight with his girlfriend. Just at the moment when he thought he had broken the grim pattern of young lives in Coney Island, Russell did something ugly: he hit his girlfriend. Terrified that she would report him to the police, that he had blown the college scholarship he was working so hard to attain, and that he would end up in prison just like his former friends, Russell climbed to the top of one of Coney Island's highest buildings. Coach Hartstein heard the news in the Lincoln cafeteria. By the time he reached the school entrance, it was crawling with police. By the time he was driven in a patrol car out to the projects, Russell was in great distress. For almost half an hour Hartstein stood fifty feet below, shouting up to Russell reassurances that he wasn't going to jail, that he still had a future in college ball. Finally Russell agreed to step back from the edge.

Since that fateful day, Russell has woken up each morning determined to atone — to show that he has outgrown such headstrong adolescent behavior and to prove to the world that he was worth saving from the edge after all. He has worked even harder in school and on the court, skipping his lunch periods to study and carrying around his vocabulary flash cards in his back pocket. Now, when Russell is finished with his afterschool errands, he goes straight home, does his push-ups, takes his vitamins, finishes his homework, and combs through college recruiting brochures until bedtime. "I want to go so far this year," he said to me one day as I dropped him off at his project building out at the end of the Coney Island peninsula. "I want everything to go right for me. There just ain't nothing in Coney Island for me no more."

•

The Empire State Games are an annual event, and this summer they are being held on and around the campus of the State University of New York at Albany. SUNY/Albany, with a student population of seventeen thousand, consists of several colossal white concrete buildings (designed by the architect who created the Kennedy Center for the Performing Arts in Washington), and organizers of the games have transformed the campus this weekend into a miniature Olympic village. Next to the university's track-and-field house stands a tremendous yellow-and-white-striped pavilion, where spectators can pick up schedules of the games. In addition to basketball, there is competition in archery, wrestling, swimming, diving, water polo, cycling, track and field, and scores of other events. Opening ceremonies feature a parade around the outdoor track by the more than five hundred participants, all of them wearing yellow nylon warm-up suits with the Empires logo. And soon the campus walkways are filled with athletes in canary yellow, walking from event to event under the hot July sun. The games themselves have taken over much of the city, and buses circulate throughout Albany bringing athletes and spectators to the various competition sites. Walking through a quiet residential area the first day to look around, I step off the curb — and am quickly pulled back on by an official — just as fifty cyclists whiz around the corner and shoot past me in a blaze of color.

Russell, Tchaka, and the other athletes will sleep in campus dormitories and eat their meals in student dining halls. Tchaka has traveled widely, even visited some college campuses as a prospective student-athlete. This, though, is one of Russell's first opportunities to get out of Coney Island and see what college life is like. At dinner the first night, Russell spots Tchaka in the food line and walks up behind him with his tray. "So, I heard you did good at Nike," he says, glancing down at Tchaka's brand-new Nike high-tops and socks. "It was lovely in Indianapolis?"

"Yeah, it was cool. We got free sneaks, played our games where the Pacers practice. And we were on TV *all* the time — it was hype." Gone are the days of Tchaka's uncertainty; he is now a veteran of the summer circuit and acts like one, responding to Russell's queries but keeping his eyes trained on the dinner options, calculating how much he can heap on his tray. As it turns out, quite a lot: turkey, stuffing, cranberry sauce, chocolate cake, chocolate milk, and Jell-O. Russell, not sure what to eat, looks at the pile on Tchaka's tray and asks for all the same things.

"Lotta coaches in the stands?" Russell inquires.

"Oh, yeah. And no slouch schools either."

"So who's recruiting you?"

"The whole Big East," Tchaka replies. "Syracuse, Providence, Villanova, Seton Hall . . ."

"You'll *never* get playing time there!" Russell says sharply. Most of the schools recruiting Russell right now are a step below the Big East, one of the nation's top college conferences, and this distinction often causes a certain tension between the teammates. "They already got power forwards," Russell goes on. "You should go to a place where they're recruiting a whole new class."

"Pipe down!" Tchaka pushes his way through the crowd of yellow-suited athletes, looking for a free table. "If you got talent, you can play anywhere." He surveys the room. "Hope the girls eat here too," he says to me. Then he turns back to Russell. "Who's recruiting *you!*"

"Rutgers, Duquesne. You see them out at Nike?"

"Who?"

"Rutgers and Duquesne!" Russell cries. "Yo, you listening to me, man?"

"Yeah, I told you, everybody was out there."

Tchaka has chosen a seat near the corner where he can watch the tide of athletes roll in. Russell immediately lowers his head and digs in; Tchaka works his way through his mountain of food but keeps an eager eye cocked. And here they are — the women's track team from New York City! Tchaka watches the runners with his mouth open and his fork suspended in midair. When an especially attractive woman settles into an empty table, Tchaka wipes his mouth, collects his tray, and immediately sets forth to introduce himself.

"Where's Tchaka going?" Russell asks me, picking up his own tray. But Tchaka spins and glares. "Why you putting on that face like you ignore us?" Russell says angrily. When Russell gets upset, his vocal cords tighten and his voice jumps to a higher register. "I hate that, nigger!" But then he catches sight of Tchaka's destination. "Oh, sorry," he mumbles, and immediately returns to his station.

Soon two other members of the New York team — Tchaka's friend from Queens, Steve Walston, and Maurice (Fresh) Brown — sit down with Russell and me. Russell returns to his food, prodding the stuffing suspiciously and bringing himself considerable grief by inquiring of his dinner companions what it is. When two women sit down at the table next to us, Steve and Maurice exchange salacious looks and jump to their feet. This time Russell stays put, finishing his meal with me. I think he's decided to ignore his teammates' antics. A few minutes later, though, Tchaka gets up to leave with his new friend, and Russell calls out to him, "Yo, bus your tray, man! Where do you think you are?" Russell, having once traveled in the company of serious delinquents, now has the zeal of the newly converted. He looks at me and frowns. "Where does he think he is?"

•

The basketball tournament is being held across town from the SUNY campus at the high school gym. Because this tournament features only players from New York State, fewer coaches fill the stands than at Nike, a national camp. But several of the schools Russell is interested in — Rutgers, Duquesne, Delaware — are in attendance. And since the Empires, unlike Nike, is open to the public, a nice crowd shows up as well. As Russell warms up for his first game, against the team from central New York, I realize that I have never actually seen him play anywhere but the Garden. And I find myself wondering how well he will maintain his composure when he's in the throes of official competition.

The New York City team has by far the most talented players in this tournament. Three of the starting five — Tchaka, Maurice Brown, and another Brooklyn player named Robert Blackwell — are newly minted Nike all-Americans. Because most of the New York players have arrived in Albany directly from other camps and tournaments, however, they have practiced as a team only once. Meanwhile, their competition, eagerly awaiting their showdown with the New York stars, have been working out in groups since May. (One kid on the Adirondack squad is said to have driven three hours to attend weekly practices.) So it is disappointing, though not a complete surprise, that in its first game New York City succumbs to a smartly executed pressing defense by Central — which all the other teams will henceforth imitate — and loses by five.

Russell rises to the occasion nonetheless, hitting his signature jump shot from everywhere on the floor. Russell in motion is a lovely sight. Moving without the ball, he stays out by the perimeter, running a slalom course past crowded, multiple picks to lose his man. Suddenly he's in the clear and snatching a crosscourt pass out of the air. When a player gets the ball in the open court, the urge to dribble is usually overwhelming, like an atavistic instinct. Players who spot up for jump shots must learn not to waste precious moments putting the ball on the floor, though the solution is not to rush one's shot either. (So many pitfalls in this game, so little time.) When Russell receives the ball, he remains preternaturally calm. His eyeballs enlarge; his eyebrows point down and in. The defender, having fought his way through the wall of picks, may hurl himself at Russell with a full-throated war cry; but Russell lifts off in his own good time, waits for the apex of his jump, then pulls the trigger. Twenty feet away the net dances on its strings.

Russell has the most complete game of any Lincoln player right now. In addition to his nearly unstoppable jump shot, he plays a fierce game of defense. Though Tchaka and Corey can outrun him, Russell practices his defensive slides — the side-to-side footwork and harassing, intrusive hand movements — with the same devotion as he does his offensive skills, and at Lincoln games Coach Hartstein always burdens him with the toughest defensive assignments. Still, to a large extent, Russell is playing this summer in the long shadow cast by Tchaka's six-foot-seven frame. When Tchaka plays well, as he did at Nike, the coaches can easily imagine a dominant presence in college. A good portion of the recruiters are here this weekend simply to pay their respects to him. (Last week Rick Barnes drove all the way to New York from Providence to watch — and be seen watching — Tchaka practice for the Empires; Tom Sullivan tried to come in from Seton Hall for the same event but his car broke down. "Tell him I tried, okay?" he said as soon as he spotted me in Albany.) But after Central wins and the New York players shuffle off to their locker room, I do hear one coach remark, "You been watching Thomas? That kid's got a helluva nice shot."

Showered and dressed, Russell and Tchaka ask me for a lift back to their dormitory. Then Steve, Maurice, and Robert show up. Out in the parking lot they all pile into my car — Russell beside me in the front, Tchaka and Robert in the back, Steve and Maurice in the far back with the hatch open and their legs hanging over the bumper. That's the entire starting line-up for New York City in one ten-year-old Toyota — more than eight hundred pounds of basketball player stuffed in the back like college freshmen filling a telephone booth. After much complaint on the part of my clutch, we achieve forward momentum, driving across Albany with the guys in the back sending their heartfelt greetings to every woman we pass. "Yo, baby, you got some *style!*"

"Man, I *hate* losing to scrub teams," Tchaka groans. "We just couldn't break their press. I was so tired by the fourth quarter, I went up for a dunk — I said yes, but my legs said no."

"That's basketball," says Maurice.

"Yeah, that's life," agrees Steve.

"Yo, Steve." Tchaka twists around, facing rear. "How come you didn't get me the rock that time I was free in the corner?" Tchaka has perfect recall of every play that should have featured him in a principal role.

"What you talking about?"

"No one was on me! I was free in the corner!"

"How'm I supposed to remember when you were free in the corner?"

"Now Fresh here" — Tchaka reaches over the back seat to slap Maurice's hand — "Fresh was feeding me alley-oops all afternoon."

"My boy!" says Maurice.

"Yo, my *man!*" cries Tchaka.

"Yo, Russell." Robert leans between the two front seats to get his teammate's attention. "You got yourself a shot!" Russell, I realize, has said almost nothing since the game ended, and he doesn't stir now. "Yo, Russell, I said you got yourself a *shot!*"

"Yeah, that's what I do," Russell replies finally. "That's my job." I glance over, and he is stroking his head, looking off.

"Yeah, well, I love to block shots," Tchaka announces. "When I hit guys, they're finished for the day."

"When I hit people, they just fall," offers Steve.

"Yeah? When I hit 'em, it's lights out."

"Mine just crumple."

"Mine don't crumple. They go *straight down.*"

Tchaka leans over to box Steve's ears, in the process clubbing Robert with his elbow. Robert shoves Tchaka. Steve whacks Maurice. All of them are hooting and slapping each other's heads, except Russell in front, still staring into space. "Hey," he says, turning to me, "did you see Rutgers where you were sitting? How about Duquesne? Those are my two schools, you know." I tell him I saw coaches from those schools and every other one he is considering, but the information doesn't lighten his mood. "I kept looking into the crowd of coaches and I think I saw them. Man, I *hope* they came. I *hope* they saw me play. It don't matter if your team loses, right? The coaches are here to look at individuals, right?" I pull into the dormitory parking lot, and the contortionists climb out the back. "Man, I *hope* they saw me play."

•

As Russell's friends, teammates, teachers, and coaches have learned over the years, it is foolish to predict what Russell's state of mind will be from one moment to the next. On his better days, he has some distance from his kaleidoscopic moods and finds the sport of guessing just what in the world is going on inside that bald head of his ("the Russell Watch," Coach Hartstein sometimes calls it) as absorbing as everyone else. Russell always keeps one college in mind that he wants to attend above all others. And after he announces that "Maryland is the only place I ever wanted to go," there will come a moment when he senses his own changeability. "Who knows what I'll say tomorrow?" he says with a laugh. "I change my mind every two days!" But then, inevitably, he stamps his foot and stubbornly declares, "I'm gonna sign with Providence as soon as I can. I don't care what anyone says — I'm *never* gonna change my mind!"

In some ways, however, Russell's delicate temperament actually makes him a pleasure to hang around; he may be moody, but he never disguises how he feels. Last spring, for example, toward the end of his junior year, Russell got word that Bobby Hartstein had been offered a college coaching job. "You can't leave!" Russell cried when he ran into Hartstein in the Lincoln corridor. "If another coach comes in, we'll take advantage of him. We'll be going crazy, I'll be taking forty shots per game!" Russell's occasional excesses with regard to shot attempts was a standing argument (and staple of amusement) between the player and the coach; and by bringing it up now, Russell was shrewdly offering Hartstein an example of what the coach would be denying himself if he left Lincoln. Russell stood in front of Hartstein, gripping the sides of his head. "You know me: I won't mean to do it, but it'll just happen!" Hartstein laughed and assured Russell that he was planning to turn the job down — in part, though he didn't say this at the time, because he felt an obligation to help steer Russell through his crucial senior year. "I just love Coach," Russell told me later. "He's always screaming, 'Russell this! Russell that!'" He shook his head and laughed. "Did you know I got voted Most Ragged-On player last year? But I didn't mind. For some reason it motivates me. I guess that's because Coach once told me, 'When I stop yelling at you, it means I don't care.'"

Russell's ability to examine his behavior and make amends for his mistakes is precisely what encourages people to go out of their way to help him — not only Hartstein, who looks out for him in a fatherly way, but also his teachers, one of whom considers Russell the hardest worker she has had during her thirty-year tenure at Lincoln. But only a few days after Russell begged Hartstein not to leave the Lincoln team, he infuriated the coach when, without any warning, he refused to show for the team's end-of-the-season dinner. The next morning Hartstein called Russell into his office for a little chat. Hartstein sat behind his desk, hands clasped in front of him, and stared up at Russell inquisitorially. Russell towered above his coach, but it seemed the reverse. "Where were you?" Hartstein demanded.

Russell averted his eyes, thrust his hands deep into his coat pockets. "My stomach hurt," he said softly.

"Yeah, so what. My stomach hurt too. You show up anyway." Russell remained silent. The wall clock ticked away like a metronome. "You didn't come because of something else," Hartstein said. "You're just not saying."

"No, Coach, I told you; my stomach hurt." Russell rubbed his belly and kept his eyes trained on the floor, but his lips twitched with the beginnings of a smile.

"If this were a playoff game, would you have shown up?" Hartstein asked.

Russell looked up and scratched his head, like a parody of a man in deepest thought, though he was clearly giving the question his usual careful consideration. "Yeah, I guess I would."

"Fine, that's what I thought. The dinner's the same thing." Hartstein shook his head and leaned down behind his desk. When he re-emerged, he was holding the two trophies Russell would have received at the dinner. "This one's for being a member of the PSAL championship team," Hartstein said evenly. "And this is for being the team's high scorer." The trophies were beautiful — elaborately layered, like wedding cakes made of brass — and when Hartstein held them out, Russell's mouth fell in open pleasure.

"They're both for me? This is *nice.* Thank you." Russell reached forward to shake his coach's hand, but Hartstein set the trophies on the desk and turned brusquely to some papers on his desk.

"I don't know why you're thanking me. If you wanted to thank me, you should have showed up for the dinner. I'm really disappointed in you. You make a commitment, you honor it. You're supposed to be one of the leaders of this team." Hartstein opened and closed desk drawers, waiting for Russell to exit. "Just think about it." Russell nodded twice and left the office without another word.

I have known Russell now for several months, and in many ways he is still a mystery to me. But one thing I am beginning to understand about him is that whenever he acts most inexplicably, it has something to do with his dream of playing college ball. For basketball, having saved Russell from the worst of the Coney Island streets, has yet to deliver him permanently from the neighborhood. And when Russell begins to doubt that it will, his fear erases the careful game plan he has designed for himself, sending him spinning in a hundred different directions. That's what happened the day he climbed to the top of the roof in Coney Island. It also may explain why he boycotted the team dinner. The day after that event, several of Russell's friends surmised that he didn't show because he knew Hartstein was going to give the Most Valuable Player award not to Russell but to a graduating senior, a slight that Russell thought might harm his recruitment chances.

In the past, Russell has tried to cope with his anxiety about securing a college scholarship by sequestering himself from all the college coaches and scouts and recruiting newsletters — everything but the game itself. For years Russell adamantly refused to play alongside Tchaka and Corey on their summer-league team, the Madison Square Boys Club in Manhattan. All the travel and pressure of summer tournament play were too much for him, and he decided he was better off practicing on his own at the Garden. But in this, the final summer season of Russell's high school career, Coach Hartstein felt that, anxious or not, the player could not afford to pass up any more exposure in front of the coaches. (It was at a Boys Club game last spring where Tchaka was first spotted by a Nike scout, leading to his invitation to the all-star camp.) Russell reluctantly agreed with Hartstein, and this summer he tried out for the Empire State Games and has worked to adopt a new attitude toward the recruiting that he dreams of and dreads in equal measure. In his mind now, Russell holds an image of a mature, knowing, and relaxed young man, handling the stress of recruiting with grace and aplomb; it is an exacting standard, and he works at all times to live up to it. "I guess it's good to come up here — you know, get my name out, get some recognition," he says in Albany, giving his scalp a quick dusting. "Basketball is a business, right? And I'm just trying to use basketball like basketball is using me." And so, steeling his nerves and determined to prove that his days of instability are behind him, he forges on with the tournament.

•

On the second day of competition, Coach Hartstein drives up from Brooklyn to watch Russell and Tchaka play. As Hartstein takes a seat next to me in the bleachers, several college coaches — following the recruiting dictum that in order to get to the kid, you've first got to get to his high school coach — immediately pack up their belongings and move next to Hartstein. "I'm afraid to go into the stands at a high school game now," Hartstein often mutters at times like this. "The coaches swarm around me like vultures — crazy!" Out on the floor, Russell hits his first two jump shots to bring New York ahead by four. Most of the coaches, though, keep their eyes on Tchaka. "You should have seen some of his moves yesterday," says Tom Sullivan of Seton Hall. "It's going to be something to see when he puts it all together." In the first few minutes, Tchaka picks up three quick fouls and has to sit down; Hartstein seizes this opportunity to steer the coaches' attention toward Russell. "You know, this kid plays such tough defense, even in pickup games, that his friends don't want to play against him in the parks," Hartstein says, to no one in particular. Sullivan can't stop talking about Tchaka, but Russell keeps lighting up the scoreboard, and soon coaches from Rutgers and Delaware are crowding Hartstein, seeking vital statistics.

"How big is Russell?" asks the Rutgers coach.

"Six-two. But he plays very big," Harstein adds quickly. "In Florida two years ago, we went up against two seven-footers. Tchaka wasn't mature enough, so I put Russell at power forward. He said, 'You want me to guard the *seven-footer*?' I said, 'Damn straight. We play man to man whoever it is.'"

Out on the court, Russell has entered the zone, as they say in this game. He's heaving in jumpers from all over the floor. Sweat streams down his face, pooling in his eyes, but he doesn't pause to mop his brow. Each time Russell sinks a shot, he runs downcourt with his hands in fists, never once cracking a smile. At one point, he catches a pass, trips over his own feet, and sinks a three-pointer while collapsing to the ground like a lame colt. Still no smile.

"You teach him that?" says the Rutgers coach, laughing.

"Yes, it's very advanced," Hartstein replies. "Freezes the defense. They figure he's gonna fall on his face, so they don't do anything. Then he scores! Heh, heh!" Nothing animates Coach Hartstein quite as much as a good performance by Russell.

"You gonna teach him to fall and hit it off the backboard?"

"That comes next."

The game ends with Russell missing on his final attempt, a twelve-footer, but New York City wins by 3, and Russell finishes with a team-high 18 points.

As Russell and his cohorts gather at the sidelines, Hartstein stands up in the bleachers, cups his hands to his mouth, and yells, "Hey, baldie! How could you have missed that last shot!" Russell looks up at the stands, his face clouded by sudden worry. "Christ, I'm kidding!" Hartstein laughs. "Don't you even know when you played a great game?" He walks down to the court and puts an arm around Russell's shoulder, speaking softly now. "Listen to me. Rutgers and a lot of Atlantic Ten schools are interested in you. You got no problems." Russell regards his coach with his usual doubtful eyes and furrowed brow. "I'm serious. If you were listed on the New York Stock Exchange, you would've posted a big gain today. You get a seven hundred on your SATs and keep doing well in class, and you'll have your pick of good colleges. So just keep doing what you're doing." Hartstein removes his arm and points a finger at Russell. "What you *should* be worrying about is getting a good night's sleep. Because if I catch you and Tchaka anywhere in Albany tonight, I'll kill you." Having dispensed his customary blend of exhortation and gruffness, Hartstein returns to the stands.

•

The New York starting five are staying in two small, adjacent dormitory rooms. Every available surface is covered with dirty basketball gear — uniforms, socks, sneakers. With the windows closed, the place smells worse than a locker room, and my eyes begin to tear as soon as I walk in. The obligatory postgame analysis begins: who dunked on whom, and how Steve once again missed golden opportunities to feed Tchaka the ball, and how Maurice felt like Michael Jordan that time he soared between two players and banked a lay-up off the glass. But winning allows for less recrimination, and soon the players are on to more pressing matters.

The campus is crawling with women, and all the guys with the exception of Russell have found dates either with other athletes or the workers in the food-service line. Steve strides in from his room across the hall, sans shirt, and begins to examine his pectoral muscles in the mirror. By his estimation, they are somewhat larger than they were this time yesterday. "You know what I hate to admit," he says. "I am *so* handsome."

"I like this life," Tchaka announces. "Travel all over the place, free food, don't gotta hear my mom's mouth every day."

Maurice elbows Steve away from the mirror and begins to examine his closely shaved scalp, turning it back and forth with his hands, as if it were a lifeless object. "Does my head look like a missile? Some girl in the dining hall just told me my head looked like a missile."

"Do my feet smell?" Tchaka asks. He picks up one of his sneakers and inserts his nose.

"Jesus, be careful, man!" Maurice cries. "Sniff too much, we'll gotta revive you for your date."

"I love taking showers," Steve declares. "Ya smell good, ya look good."

"One hand washes the other" — Maurice has a proverb for everything — "both hands wash the face."

"You know," Russell says. "That pasta server downstairs *was* cute. I think I'll go find out what she's doing tonight."

"Yeah, Russell!" everyone cries.

Russell has been standing in the on-deck circle, and now it's his turn to step up to the mirror. "Tchaka, can you see this zit?" he asks.

"Nah, you're fine."

"No, I think you can definitely see it. Stand over there. Can you see it now?"

"The zit is *fine!*"

Russell puts on a clean white sweatshirt. "How 'bout this speck of dirt on the sleeve?" he asks. There is much imitation of the squeak that registers in Russell's voice when he speaks in earnest, but Russell won't be shamed out of a thorough pre-date examination of zits, specks, and other assorted imperfections. "I can't get it out. Can you see it from over there?"

"Yo, just chill, Russell! Chill, chill, chill!"

"I'm chill, I'm chill!" Russell says, his voice rising up the scale.

The time for deep perusal is over, and Tchaka, Steve, Maurice, and Robert all stream noisily out the door and down the stairs, leaving Russell and me alone in the room. He's still examining his sleeve; I can tell he's going to ask me about it. But he gives it up and smiles — maybe for the first time all weekend. "You think that pasta server will go out with me tonight?" Russell asks. (I do; she will.) He grabs his new baseball cap and puts it on sideways. "I'm fly," he says. "I'm a fly guy." Then he runs outside to catch up with his roving friends.

•

This is how Russell happens to arrive at the foul line with seven tenths of a second to go in his team's game against Western. For three quarters, New York City has played with its usual bruising intensity, but by the start of the fourth quarter, Western begins to apply the press, and once again the New Yorkers are getting unhinged. Normally Tchaka, Maurice, Steve, and Robert play with aggressiveness, but for some reason they all stop attacking the basket today, which is the only way to make a pressing team pay for its sins.

Then, as he has done all weekend, Russell takes matters into his own hands. From everywhere on the floor and whenever he touches the ball, Russell shoots. This is the sort of behavior that can annoy a teammate. Robert, having complimented Russell on his shot that first day, grew noticeably irritated the next day as he looked at the stats and read, "Thomas: Shot attempts: 50." But when you sink all your shots in quick succession, as Russell does now — a dazzling, multiradial barrage, like a billiard player on a streak — it tends to silence your critics. Russell pours in something like 10 points in the final minutes. But with less than five seconds to go, New York City is still down, 87 to 83. And even as Russell heaves up his final three-point attempt from deep behind the line, the crowd is already cheering a Western victory. But just after the ball falls through the hoop yet again, bringing New York to within one, a whistle blows. A Western player has committed the sport's one unforgivable sin: with less than a second to go in a game that should be history, he fouls Russell away from the ball, sending New York's best marksman to the line for two shots: one to tie, one to win.

So which Russell Thomas will show up at the foul line now? The one who steals out of locker rooms and boycotts team meetings, and sometimes dissolves altogether in the face of the college-recruiting pressure; or the player who has taken a risk simply by showing up this weekend and has played each game with the kind of fortitude and resolve that all great deeds require? Perhaps the coach of the Western team is wondering this too, for just as Russell walks to the line and the other players gather beneath the basket . . . the coach calls a time-out. This is standard procedure in college and the NBA, the idea being that a sixty-second interval may throw the player off his rhythm and give him time to choke. But there is something gratuitous about it here, in a summer tournament that is, at bottom, an exhibition staged for the benefit of the kids.

Russell's team troops toward its bench, Russell following two steps behind. Then, as the New York team forms its huddle, Russell does an odd thing: with the game hanging in the balance, he breaks from the group and wanders to the opposite end of the bench, where he picks up his new baseball cap. Evidently it still needs breaking in, for Russell begins working the bill — lovingly, scientifically — to give it the proper curve. As he does so, the atmosphere in the gym suddenly shifts, as it does in any crowded locale when something of unusual interest — a celebrity, or a man having a heart attack — is discovered in its midst. The babble of a dozen conversations ends in a hush; heads turn to the one spot. Even some of Russell's teammates stand with mouths agape as Russell, about to shoot the most important foul shots in his young life, becomes raptly engaged with his baseball cap. For several long moments much of the arena is transfixed by the sight and by the mystery of it too. Is this a display of anxiety that bodes ill for the task at hand? Or is Russell concentrating so fiercely that he has shut out everything that usually distracts him — the crowd, the coaches, all his worries about his future?

The buzzer sounds, ending the time-out. Russell looks up, as if stirred from a reverie, and carefully places his cap on a chair. From one side of the bench, his teammates walk diagonally toward the basket to resume their positions at the rebound line. From the other side, Russell heads the opposite way toward the foul line. Just as he and his teammates are about to converge, Russell slows, as if at a curb to let the traffic pass. Then he sets himself at the foul line. The ref hands him the ball. Russell bounces it five times. Tchaka walks over to him and gives him those words of advice, to which Russell says nothing in return. And then, without further ado and still giving no clue as to whether he is calm or terrified, Russell tosses in both foul shots to win the game.

As befits the moment, euphoria breaks out among the New York City squad. Tchaka, Maurice, Steve, and Robert jump for joy, punching the air, slapping Russell all over. Hartstein bounds to his feet, yelling, "That's my kid! The one who just won the game on the foul line? That's my kid!" Several college coaches smile with the satisfaction of having watched a great game, their instincts as fans awakened in them after long hibernation. In his long march toward a college scholarship, Russell has just passed an important milestone. And this is how he salutes himself: he retrieves his cap, picks some lint from the bill, and shuffles off alone while his teammates continue to celebrate on his behalf.

•

On Sunday morning, in front of a thin crowd, New York loses the championship game to Central and takes the silver medal. Once again my car doubles as a compression chamber as I drive the loose-limbed boys back to Brooklyn. Halfway down the New York State Thruway, I pull into a rest area so that we can get some drinks and stretch ourselves. When I return from the men's room, I see Russell off by the side of the road, toes up against the white line. What the hell is he up to now? I join him and find him already worrying about the next few weeks of his summer. He will take a summer school course at Lincoln to get some extra credits, he tells me. He will continue to study each night for his SATs. "I'm also planning a new image for myself when the school year starts," he says in his enigmatic fashion. "And you know what else? I'm gonna dunk this year too." For years, I knew, Russell had earned a reputation in Coney Island for "playing white" — taking a lay-up when he could have dunked, that sort of thing. "No one thinks I can dunk 'cause I never dunked in public," he says. "But between you and me, I dunk in the park all the time — when no one's looking." I am tempted to ask him whether this is some sort of riddle: Is a dunk really a dunk if no one is around to see it? But Russell isn't smiling; he's looking straight ahead, squinting through the road dust kicked up by the passing cars. "I'm gonna dunk this year," he says grimly, giving me to understand that dunking — like everything else he has accomplished this weekend — is merely an item that must be checked off on his list of "Things to Do to Get My Scholarship." "Trust me on this one," he says again. "I'm gonna dunk." And after having watched him for the last four days, I do.

Four

"THE CROWD was hyped to my surprise, as I looked in the gym with my own two eyes. The game had started with a lot of funk. Two minutes later, there goes a dunk. A push, a shove, a foul, a score; the crowd was yelling out, 'More more more!' Tension grew fast; the game got rough. A war of the best and all that stuff. A shot went up; my man grabbed the pill. Slowly I caught it as the fans yelled, 'Chill!' But as the gym got silent without a sound, everyone watched as *I threw it down!*"

Corey looked up from his three-ring binder, his mellifluous voice still sounding in the air. "You liked that, didn't you." He grinned at me. "I wrote that in about ten minutes." Corey was sitting in the back row of an empty classroom at Lincoln High wearing a purple linen sports jacket with narrow lapels over a snowy white T-shirt. Against the gray classroom walls, he stood out like a peacock in a vacant lot. The team's mandatory study hall had just ended, and throughout the period I had been watching Corey. For a kid whose lousy grades always kept alive the threat of ineligibility, Corey never seemed to waste a minute of study hall. All hell might be breaking loose — players firing spitballs at each other or jumping from desk to desk — but Corey always sat in the last row in his finery, bent over his desk, hard at work. One day I asked him what he had been able to accomplish amid such havoc and he read me "I Threw It

Down," his latest creation. "I'm going to be a writer," he said, stacking his books and heading to the locker room for practice. "You know — creative writing, poetry, free-associative stuff." He shrugged. "I just play ball to take up time."

Actually, it might be more accurate to say that Corey approaches basketball in the same way he does poetry and fashion — as an occasion for self-expression. I remember the first day I spent any time with him. I had gone to Queens to watch him and Tchaka play with the Madison Square Boys Club in a summer tournament. Driving back to Coney Island afterward, we got stuck in a traffic jam during the hottest part of the day. Tchaka, nursing a thirty-two-ounce bottle of Coke in the front seat, grew snappish and tense in the withering heat; but Corey stretched out in the back and began a monologue about the game. "Felt *good* today . . . Guess I had my flying license with me . . . Man, those guys fouled me so much it felt like they were playing a game of cards on my back . . . What did they do — pick that ref up at a local bar? . . . You didn't catch that last dunk of mine? I guess your eyes were too slow." Corey kept up such a steady flow of one-liners that Tchaka was soon doubled over with laughter and the related complication of having his Coke stream out his nose.

"You know why basketball is so great?" Corey said to me on another occasion. "'Cause there's just no limit to what you can do. Everything goes." I wasn't certain what he was getting at until I saw him later that day at practice. Inspired by the crowd of students and teachers that sometimes showed up to watch, Corey drove toward the basket and went airborne in the customary fashion — bellowing and slamming the ball violently between his hands. But instead of jamming it, Corey rolled the ball daintily off his fingertips into the hoop — a dunk in the ironic mode. "Jesus, did you see Corey lift off?" said one spectator. "What-

ever he's wearing, I want a pair." Corey overheard this remark and said, "You like that? Stay right there. More to
come." And there was. "Do the three-sixty!" someone yelled
from the bleachers, and Corey blanched: "The three-sixty?
I'll kill myself. But okay." And he performed a gorgeous,
gyrating dunk. "Statue of Liberty!" came the next request,
and Corey took off near the foul line, soared toward the
basket, and then — legs split, arm extended, ball held high
like a torch — threw down a thunderous, backboard-rattling
jam.

At a time in life when most teenagers seek to imitate the
behavior of their peers, Corey is constantly initiating his
own trends. He often arrives for practice as unconvention-
ally attired as he is in the classroom — a yellow sweatshirt
with the sleeves and collar scissored away or standard-issue
sweatpants rolled halfway up his thighs like Huck Finn.
Then, while his teammates warm up with a few laps around
the gym, Corey will run backward or stand at center court
doing tricks with a jump rope. When the team runs wind
sprints on the tree-lined outdoor track, Corey will gladly
volunteer for the outside lane so that he can run his hands
luxuriously through the canopy of leaves above his head.
Corey usually remains alone in these diversions, and happily so, but one time a few years ago he did encourage all
his teammates to show up at practice just like him — without socks. The memory of Coach Hartstein's stunned reaction still gives him enormous pleasure. Corey's eyes bulge
in perfect imitation of Hartstein *in extremis: "Goddamnit,
guys! Where the hell are your socks?"*

•

Corey relies on his good humor and even temperament to
see him through many of life's travails, like getting fouled
so hard on the way to the hoop that he lands on his head
("Hey," he says, still supine and clutching his skull, "does

it get any better than this?") or the sound of gunfire just outside his project ("In Coney Island, it's always the Fourth of July"). And it appears to be in evidence when he arrives by bus with Russell at the B/C All-Stars camp in Gettysburg, Pennsylvania. The sight of so many players and coaches crammed into the gym at Gettysburg College turns Russell's stomach, but Corey says, "Walk in the park. This should be a walk in the park."

B/C is not an exclusive, invitational affair like Nike, nor a tournament requiring try-outs like the Empires. B/C is a purely profit-making enterprise: anyone who can afford the camp's $300 fee is welcome to put on a numbered jersey and play for four days. And with the help of talented players like Corey and Russell, whom the camp lures with a half-price offer, B/C is able to attract scores of Division I coaches and, in turn, hundreds of less talented campers who want to play in front of those coaches, though they don't stand a chance of getting recruited and are charged the camp's full fee.

Besides their desire for exposure, Corey and Russell also attend B/C every summer in the hope of escaping the Coney Island streets and the New York heat. But the camp this year doesn't offer much relief. Someone has just estimated the gym temperature at about 95 degrees, so four standing fans have been brought in and stationed at the corners. It's no use, though, not with so many bodies warming the place. This year an astonishing four hundred players have arrived from up and down the East Coast, dreaming of Division I scholarships, and camp administrators have them jammed together in two small gyms — sixty players running back and forth on six side-by-side courts, and another couple of hundred campers standing on the sidelines, waiting their turn.

Players arrive by bus, change in the hallway, and begin playing moments later. (Corey is still pulling on his jersey when someone passes him the ball.) And because the courts are so close together, no one can tell where the out-of-bounds lines are, nor distinguish one referee's whistle from another. Players on adjacent courts keep colliding and tripping over guys on the sidelines. In the first day, so many players suffer injuries that the camp turns the college weight room into a first-aid station: kids, pale with dehydration, lie on the bench presses clutching water bottles. A row of campers hold ice packs to their knees, swollen from six games a day played on floors that simulate concrete. A camp staffer stands at the door practicing triage: "Okay, guys, get your ice and move to the back." On the sidelines, the coaches stand only a few feet behind the players, and not all of them worry about NCAA rules barring contact between coach and player during the camp season; the recruiting is going on right here, spilling through the gym's steel doors onto the parking lot. Every time I walk out there to get some air, I see a coach or two backing players up against their car doors, leaning amorously toward the recruits. It resembles a local pickup scene, except in this case the lust to score is more intense.

B/C is one of dozens of privately run basketball camps throughout the country. Every summer, there is a move to clean up the camp scene, which everyone agrees is a mess, but no one knows precisely what to do about it. Because school isn't in session, the Board of Education can't look out for players like Russell and Corey when they go off to camp; and because the players are not yet in college, the NCAA has little jurisdiction over what happens to them, except to prohibit its own coaches from speaking to the players. That leaves the kids in the hands of the summer camp directors, who do not represent the most reform-minded element of the high school basketball business. On one end are the shoe companies like Nike, dispensing their brand-name sneakers with something other than charity in mind. On the other end are the private camps like B/C, charging players exorbitant fees while opening the doors to any recruiter, scout, or street agent who happens to come along. Recently the NCAA threatened to shut down all private enterprises and create its own set of regional summer basketball camps. If that occurs, however, camps like B/C will most certainly launch a restraint-of-trade lawsuit. In a business in which everyone is hungering for a piece of these kids, why should the NCAA possess the only hunting license? In the meantime, if you've got dreams of getting recruited to college, a camp like B/C is the place to go.

With such a congestion of bodies in the Gettysburg College gym, it takes me some time to locate Russell and Corey, but when I do I can see immediately why the camp considers them such a draw. I watch Russell's game for twenty minutes, and for twenty minutes he doesn't miss a shot. The coaches are crowding along the sidelines, watching. But this doesn't seem to cheer him any more than it did at the Empires. Each time he sinks a shot, he runs downcourt casting furtive glances at the sidelines, trying to determine whether his favorite schools are represented in the crowd.

Corey, too, has drawn a sizable group of coaches. He doesn't have Russell's finely honed skills nor Tchaka's height, so the coaches interested in him are more likely to be from Bowling Green, Fordham, and Saint Peter's than from the Big East or the Atlantic 10. Nevertheless, Corey tries to make up in style and speed what his game sometimes lacks in substance. At six feet one, Corey is so fast he doesn't even bother to fake; he just wastes his man on the first step and springs into the air as if coming off a trampoline. Corey is one of the most unselfish players I have seen, and for a while at B/C he seems content just setting the table for his teammates. But what a way to set the table. Corey drives downcourt with such swashbuckling abandon that his teammates stand and gape while his passes slip through their fingers or bounce off their heads. So Corey starts taking it to the hoop each time himself, yelling to his own teammates, "*Get out my way!*" The kid guarding Corey can't figure out how to stop him in any legally defensible manner, so he grabs hold of Corey's jersey, going along for the ride. At camps like these, the slow-footed players all want to take on the New York City stars, and the refs don't seem to care unless blood is drawn. So Corey, mugged each time he ventures into the paint, finishes his plays by turning toward the official with one eyebrow raised and his hands up by his shoulders, seeking restitution.

"Damn, there's just no air in here!" After his final game of the day, Corey stumbles out to the parking lot and grips the gym door for support. "I don't like that. I don't like not to breathe." Corey takes pride in keeping in superb shape; even during the fiercest competition he comports himself as though he were playing in top hat and tails. However, he has also never played in an oven before. He collapses to the ground, his chest heaving. "You see my game? You see my teammates?" he pants. "I'm playing with beginners! I try to understand. I pass it to them right where they want it, but it hits them in the head! These guys are loafs. *Bread loafs.*" Catching his breath, Corey picks up a pebble and skips it across the asphalt. "It's hard to keep yourself up, you know, with teammates like this. I try, I try, but if this doesn't change, I'm gonna need some therapy." Noticing that I've stopped writing in my notebook, Corey nods for me to pick up my pen again. "And the guys we're playing against?" he continues, finishing his postgame interview and mocking the ritual of it at more or less the same time, "I would say this about them. I would say they're animals!" Corey raises his hands in surrender. "At this point I'm just trying not to get hurt. Some kid was actually hanging on my leg. I said, 'Excuse me? Is this the kissing game?'" Corey swivels his head back and forth, conversing with himself. "'No, we call this game basketball.'" Corey as kindergarten teacher: "'Can you say *basketball?*'"

The gym doors swing open and Russell appears, weaving unsteadily on his pins. He looks equally spent, but finds less humor in it than his friend does. "Man, my team *stinks*. We haven't won a game all day," he says, sinking to the ground beside us. Russell arrived in Gettysburg determined to stay calm about the camp scene, but his worst fantasies — and there were many of them — didn't prepare him for B/C. "To tell you the truth," Russell says, "I wouldn't mind getting this all over with. Yeah, soon as I pass my SATs, I think I'm gonna sign early with Rutgers. Just gimme that piece of paper, boy, and I'll sign right now. 'Cause I can't take any more of this camp shit." He looks at Corey and offers a casual chuckle, but it's tinged with something close to hysteria. "Later for this, right?"

After the two of them have rested for a while, we walk over to the college dormitory where Corey and Russell have been assigned to bunk with three other campers — "just like roaches and rats," Corey remarks serenely as they enter the room. Russell doesn't move to take off his uniform; he stands by his bed, hands heavy at his sides. But Corey peels off his clothes, takes a quick shower, and flips on his boom box as he towels himself off. D.J. Jazzy Jeff and the Fresh Prince fill the air. "That's better," Corey announces, stretching out on his bed wrapped in a wet towel. "A nice cool shower and some relaxing music." Lying there, he raps along for a while: *"Back in Philly we'd be out in the park. Guys out huntin' and girls doin' likewise, honkin' at the honey in front of you with the light eyes."* He props his hands behind his head: *"She turns around to see what you beepin' at. It's like the summer's a natural aphrodisiac."* Finally he closes his eyes: *"It's late in the day and I ain't been on the court yet. Hustle to the mall to get me a short set."* Every minute or so he interrupts the Fresh Prince to let out an indulgent sigh — "Aaaaah" — and to mumble "Loafs. Bread loafs." Then the strain of the day leaves his face and his breathing becomes shallow and regular. Corey may cherish his ability to rap and rhyme, but evidently he doesn't let it interfere with a good nap.

•

A week later, we're all back in Coney Island. Russell starts his evening workouts at the Garden again, clearly relieved that the summer season is winding down. Corey sometimes shows up, too, but usually in shades and street shoes, and then wanders off alone to pursue his other interests. As much as he hates Coney Island, Russell often feels uncomfortable away from his home turf, but Corey goes club-hopping in Manhattan and every time he shows up for a game — no matter where in the city it is — some girl he dated in the long-forgotten past recognizes him and starts shrieking out his name. Corey's shrewdness on a variety of topics — basketball, rapping, writing poetry, dating, fashion, churchgoing, and cooking — has earned him the nickname Future, because, as Russell once explained to me, "Corey's a future-type guy, crazy-smart, a walking genius. There are no limits to what he can do."

Nevertheless, the infrequency of Corey's appearances on the Coney Island courts this summer is giving rise to speculation over just how much he wants that college scholarship after all. No one expects Corey to be as highly recruited as Tchaka or Russell, but he too might have made the cut for the Empire State Games if he hadn't missed the second try-out. And he certainly would have made the B/C camp's all-star game on the final day if he had paid his discounted fee on time. (Coach Hartstein had even sent the money.) Corey is starting to get a reputation in Coney Island as a little "lost in the sauce" and "too cute for his own good," caring less about the quality of the college he will attend next year than whether it offers an acceptable male-female ratio. On a team where playing unselfishly is considered the best way never to get recruited, Corey often baffles his friends by ignoring wide-open shots if he sees an exotic pass to be made. And Corey has yet to live down a heretical incident that occurred last year in one of the season's crucial games. Corey was all alone under the basket, tried a fancy lay-up, and blew it. Coach Hartstein and his two assistants rose to their feet, howling in rage. As Corey jogged down-court, he shrugged, palms turned toward the ceiling. "Relax, guys," he said, nonchalance itself. "It's just basketball."

But measuring Corey's ambition is a complicated business. He once had a beautiful jumper to complement his slashing, ball-to-the-basket game, which made him a threat inside and out. And some Coney Islanders believe that the only thing preventing Corey from signing with a high Division I school is his refusal to practice that shot, which now comes and goes depending upon his concentration. Yet Corey is not undisciplined. In practice, he is often the only player to execute Coach Hartstein's drills perfectly on the first try. He never gets caught in a game going the wrong way on one of the team's set plays — and anyone who does is found by Corey to possess a "weak mind." Even his penchant for distributing the ball to his teammates has a certain deliberateness to it. "Maybe I *have* given up my shooting game a bit," he acknowledged to me down at B/C. "But everybody on this team is always arguing about not getting their shots. So I'll pass the ball just to keep everyone from fighting so much. Not everyone agrees with me. All my friends be saying, 'Shoot! Shoot!' every time I touch the ball. But this is my team, and I'll do what I want." Some of Corey's friends think he may be too amiable for his own good.

Perhaps the one person who understands Corey best is his brother Willie. The Johnsons are one of the few stable, intact families I know in Coney Island. Corey is the second youngest of eight children, all raised by a mother and father who still live at home. Corey's father, Bill Johnson, earns a decent living running his own plumbing business; I often see him driving around the neighborhood, waving cheerfully from his van. And though they live in the Coney Island projects, among families in this neighborhood the Johnsons are considered relatively fortunate.

One day, curious to hear his thoughts about Corey, I went looking for Willie Johnson. Willie is only twenty-one years old and he often wears a black mesh tank top, the better to display his impressive physique and the tattoo of a dragon on his arm. But he has a quiet, considered way of talking that belies his youth. Like all the Johnson boys, Willie played varsity ball in high school. After he scored 1100 on his SATs — the highest in anyone's memory — he became the Lincoln team's in-house tutor and had his pick of college programs. Instead, he decided to go into business for himself as a barber. And business at his shop, across town in the Flatbush section of Brooklyn, is now thriving.

Willie's shop is on the second floor of a commercial building just off Flatbush Avenue, but Willie has given it a homey feel. Taped to the mirrors are photos of the extensive Johnson clan — Corey, Willie, and their six siblings. A T-shirt commemorating Lincoln's championship last year is pinned to the wall, next to a painting of Jesus, a bust of Nefertiti, and four portraits of Martin Luther King. Willie has also slapped up an assortment of bumper stickers that seem to represent a range of interests among the Johnsons: MORE HUGGING, LESS MUGGING and TO ALL YOU VIRGINS . . . THANKS FOR NOTHING.

"I made it and I'm doing all right. But I'm fortunate, considering I didn't go to college," Willie says to me. "Most of the guys who didn't go to school — well, they ain't doing as well." He pushes a broom across the barbershop floor, collecting masses of cut hair. "That's why I been telling Corey, 'You *got* to go to school; you *got* to go to college.' I say to him, 'You want to be a writer? That's cool. But how you gonna do that if you don't go to college?'" Willie frowns. "'And how you gonna go to college if the coaches never see what you can do with a basketball?' I talk and talk, but to tell you the truth, I'm not sure how much he been listening."

Corey's assiduous cultivation of his image as the team's philosopher-king often keeps adults at arm's length. Any other kid on the Lincoln varsity who courted such academic trouble, as Corey did last spring, would have received a withering tongue-lashing from Hartstein. But Corey is so dignified and aristocratic that adults sometimes keep their distance, if only because they can't quite believe that someone as obviously smart as Corey could be screwing up the way he is.

Willie stops sweeping for a moment and props his broomstick beneath his arm. "To tell you the truth, I think Corey cares more about his recruiting than he's letting on. He just don't think it's cool to show how much. But you don't play as hard as Corey does if you don't care." I mention to Willie something I had recently learned from Tchaka: that Corey, who still hasn't seen his recruiting mail because Coach Hartstein wants his grades to improve first, apparently sneaks a peek at Hartstein's school mailbox to see whether he's getting any letters. When Willie hears this, his eyes light up. "See, I *told* you he cares," he says with a laugh. Then he grows serious again and nods, once, to himself. "I'm going to have to have a little talk with Corey *real soon*."

Five

NOSTALGIA ASIDE, it is fair to say that few New York neighborhoods have changed as radically over the years as Coney Island. In the early 1900s, of course, Coney Island was known primarily as an immigrant destination, as boat-loads of Jewish, Irish, and Italian families found homes in the neighborhood, moving side by side into the two-story bungalows, with gardens in front and porches out back, that covered the peninsula from end to end. That was also the heyday of the great Coney Island amusement parks — Stee-plechase, Luna, and Dreamland — famous not only for the technological wizardry of their rides and exhibits but also for the utopian ideas that inspired them: that in this bur-geoning, polyglot city, where the lines of ethnicity and class were being drawn ever more indelibly, there might exist at least one place where urban discord gave way to the happy carnival scene of Ferris wheels and roller coasters, romance and Nathan's franks. Every day, for a nickel fare, New York's new subway system brought millions of people to Coney Island. "Nowhere else in the United States will you see so many races mingle in a common purpose for a common good," wrote a local historian. "Democracy meets here and has its first interim skin to skin."

Today, Coney Island displays the results of a different ex-periment in city living: urban renewal. The neighborhood's transformation began in the late 1950s. By then, European immigration had slowed, and all but a few amusement park rides had vanished, victims of suburbanization and the auto craze that sent New Yorkers spinning northward for their leisure. City officials, desperately in need of affordable housing, bulldozed block after block of multifamily homes in Coney Island, and over the next twenty years erected in their place one of the largest collections of federal, state, and local housing projects in the city. Whenever the housing authority needed to relocate poor black families from another New York neighborhood, Coney Island made itself available: a thirty-square-block area devoted to nothing but high-rise apartment buildings.

Blacks did not gravitate to Coney Island naturally, as they did to Harlem and Bedford-Stuyvesant, the city's two largest African-American communities. Among the row houses and tenements of Harlem and Bed-Stuy, one feels a connection both to midtown Manhattan, an easy commute, and to other black neighborhoods nearby. But there is nothing whatsoever near the Coney Island projects — for all intents and purposes the end of the line. Coney Island is the end of Ocean Parkway, Brooklyn's principal thoroughfare, which traverses the entire alphabetical grid of the borough's streets before crossing Avenue Z and plunging into the shadow of the highrises. Coney Island is also the end of four different subway lines, each originating some thirty miles to the north and terminating on elevated tracks just blocks away from Nathan's and the Atlantic Ocean. And Coney Island, of course, is also the end of New York City. Surrounded on three sides by water, and cut off on the fourth by the great ethnic divide of Brighton Beach, the Coney Island peninsula feels like a separate territory, as removed from the rest of New York as Guam. City officials have grown accustomed to treating the neighborhood that way. During the urban-renewal years, Coney Island became a dumping ground, the terminus of forced migrations for hundreds of black families who were pushed to the sea.

Just to get to Coney Island from Manhattan requires an hour-long subway ride, since few of the neighborhood's residents own cars, and then a mile-long walk out to the projects. And once tenants arrive at the end of the peninsula, home to the largest concentration of buildings, they find none of the amenities that New Yorkers take for granted; there are no supermarkets or public libraries, no police precincts or hospitals, no restaurants or nightclubs. The streets offer none of the bustling commerce and pedestrian life that are the great compensations for city living. In fact, for many long stretches one sees nothing but slate-gray project buildings, vacant lots, and basketball courts. Despite the concentration of tenants in each building, the project courtyards and walkways often look emptied-out, as if all but the drug dealers have been put under curfew or quarantine. In this desolate, urban-lunar landscape, one doesn't even come across many unfamiliar faces; no one simply passes through Coney Island on the way to somewhere else.

Unmoored as it is from the rest of New York, Coney Island has found some compensation for its isolation by evolving into one of New York's most closely knit African-American communities. Although I failed to see them during my first few visits there, several informal networks exist in Coney Island to help defend the neighborhood against the forces of anomie. There is the Coney Island Gospel Assembly on Neptune Avenue, which draws large crowds every Sunday. There are the recreational centers on the ground floors of many project buildings, which provide small islands of community. And above all there is the neighborhood's faith in, and sponsorship of, the game of basketball.

Basketball is so inextricably woven into the fabric of Coney Island life that almost everyone in this neighborhood has grown up playing the game or following the fortunes of those who do. Huge crowds show up to watch the summer tournament games at the Garden, and almost everyone can recite a complete oral history of the neighborhood's great players — a remarkable number, too, considering the actual size of Coney Island. There was Eric (Spoon) Marbury and Norman (Jou-Jou) Marbury, Stephon's older brothers; Dwayne (Tiny) Morton and Carlton (Silk) Owens; Bernard (T) Mitchell and David (Chocolate) Harris. People remember the exact scores of games played at the Garden more than ten years ago, or describe in rapturous detail the perfect arc that Silk Owens put on his jumper before he was shot in the elbow in 1982. Videos of Lincoln games are circulated from apartment to apartment, and dog-eared copies of a ten-year-old University of Georgia catalogue, with a picture of Spoon Marbury playing with future NBA great Dominique Wilkins, get passed around the neighborhood like samizdat.

Every summer night, as soon as the day's heat begins to break, the Garden fills with players at their devotions; and the code of conduct that governs activities there is more rigorous than I have seen at any other Coney Island court or, for that matter, any other neighborhood in New York City. Players sometimes get into shape for the summer season by playing full-court one-on-one while their compatriots watch from the sidelines, cheering them on. It is not unusual to find guys falling into two ruler-straight lines to practice lay-ups and crosscourt passing. One day I walked by the Garden while ten players halted all competition to work on a double-down defensive rotation and to trade tips on the most effective way of handling the backcourt trap. Some of the neighborhood elders serve as free-lance coaches to the younger kids, and during games at the Garden players actually heed their coaches' sideline instructions — especially during the summer tournaments, which are often better organized than games in the PSAL. During tournament play, everyone pitches in to buy team T-shirts and trophies — even to hire a ref and to persuade him, against his better judgment, to stay out at the Coney Island courts and officiate the games until they conclude, usually sometime past two A.M.

The neighborhood's most revered free-lance coach is a longtime Coney Island resident named Robert Williams. Most weekdays around six o'clock his tall, lanky frame comes into view a couple of blocks from the Garden. He often wears a pair of dark blue overalls and a threadbare baseball cap, and he trudges with heavy steps across the vacant lots, the neighborhood dogs barking at his heels. At Mermaid Avenue, the traffic slows his march, and he pauses at the corner to remove his cap and wipe the sweat from his forehead. Then he arranges a cheerful expression on his face, climbs through the hole in the Garden fence, and greets the assembled players, all of whom call him (though no one can ever remember why) Mr. Lou.

During the day, Mr. Lou does maintenance work at a local nursing home. His second job begins at dusk when he sits down on the Garden asphalt, both legs stretched in front of him and his arms propped behind, as if he were sunning himself on a dock. I have heard players refer to Mr. Lou affectionately as "the old man who's dope." In fact, he is not yet fifty, but his beard is flecked with gray; his measured speech, amid the hip-hop cadences of the street, sounds full of gravity; and the expression in his eyes as he watches the youthful players often takes on an inscrutable sadness. In this neighborhood of teenage mothers and absent fathers, he seems like the wise Buddha himself set down for meditation at center court.

One evening in late August, Mr. Lou comes by the Garden at his usual time to observe Russell, Corey, and some other players in a half-court practice. The season when the cool sea breezes of early summer offered relief to the players is just a memory. Now it's hot — *God, is it hot.* Even by eight o'clock, the 90-degree heat hasn't broken, and the soggy, membranous air doesn't stir. Last week the temperature climbed so high in Coney Island that the street alongside the Garden cracked right open, like a volcano. No one expects city repair crews to fill in the crater for months, so people have begun using it as a Dumpster — chairs, tires, bags of trash are piling up, and the stray dogs and occasional sea gulls nose around, searching for food. Even in this tropical weather the players come out each night. But in the aquarium light of dusk, in the heat waves shimmering above the Garden asphalt, they move languidly through the resistant air, as if they were playing their game under water.

Mr. Lou is pleased that Corey is making one of his rare Garden appearances tonight and hopes he can persuade the elusive player to work on his outside shot. "Corey had a beautiful jumper, but he's given it up," Mr. Lou says to me as we search without luck for a patch of cool asphalt. "I have no idea why. That kid's a mystery." Russell, on the other hand, openly hungers for the attention of his coaches, especially Mr. Lou, whom he listens to with his brow furrowed in concentration. It was Mr. Lou who suggested a few months ago that Russell practice shooting from a chair, and after that bit of advice, unorthodox though it may have been, Russell began drilling his stationary jump shot every time. But whenever Russell shoots off the dribble, some glitch in his mechanics causes a misfire, so he's asked Mr. Lou to come out this evening to render a diagnosis.

Mr. Lou watches Russell in motion for a couple of minutes, head cocked to one side as if he might actually hear the defect. Finally he says, "Yup, you should be housing that." The instant Mr. Lou speaks, the game stops and all the players turn inquiringly in his direction. "Squaring up. That's your problem. You're not squaring up." Mr. Lou holds both index fingers in the air to diagram the position Russell's body should take when he leaves the ground. Russell looks at him without comprehension. "You're staggering around like a drunk, Russell. When you come off that pick and get the ball, don't weave all over the place like a wino. You got to go straight up. Straight up. Try it now. Remember: straight up." Mr. Lou claps his hands twice, and the players, lulled by his hypnotic counsel, jolt back to life. The game resumes. Mr. Lou inclines his head toward mine. "Now's the perfect time of day for this," he whispers. "In the evening, in this heat, they're dog tired, and that's just about the only time they'll listen."

As the players run through their paces, Mr. Lou calls out in a spirited baritone, "Fight through that pick! . . . C'mon, you ever heard of boxing out? . . . Don't be intimidated! . . . Where's your defensive rotation? . . . That's just about the laziest pass I ever did see . . . *Move without the ball, damnit!*" Russell does just that. He comes off a high pick, catches a crosscourt pass, takes two dribbles, and plants his right foot, hard, on the blacktop. When he jumps this time, his body rises straight up. "Cash. Count it," Mr. Lou announces before Russell has released the ball. As it spins through the net, players on both teams give Russell a hand.

Mr. Lou grew up in Coney Island and attended Lincoln High, where he played football in the early sixties. He went on to play in the semipro league, but a leg injury prematurely ended his athletic career. A dozen years ago, he began coaching the basketball players at the Garden. "You'll hear a lot of trash talk about kids like these," he says softly so that the players won't hear. "But I've learned that as long as you work with them and show them you care, they care. They all want to learn the game, go to college, make something of their lives. I tell them, one bad injury can tear up your whole career, but no one can take away your brain.

And they listen because it's the truth, and around here the kids don't hear the truth a lot."

In his counseling endeavors, Mr. Lou has picked up a sidekick of sorts, another free-lance coach named David Reed, who goes by the *nom de court* of Disco Dave. At twenty-nine, Disco still has the thick arms and shoulders that powered his playground game, but his belly is beginning to slacken from a gourmand's appreciation of all foods artificial. During the day Disco works at the community center next to the Garden. After hours he picks up a bag or two of Cheese Doodles at the bodega on Mermaid and tours the neighborhood courts, gathering fresh evidence for his argument that the Coney Island projects breed the finest basketball players in all of New York City.

"I can watch a ten-year-old walk across the court and know instantly whether he's got the Coney Island game," Disco declares one evening as we cruise through the Garden, then Run-and-Gun Land, then Chop-Chop Land so that I might have the opportunity to judge for myself how indisputably right he is. "And if you don't got game, take your smack out of Coney Island! Because we only got room for the best. All the great Brooklyn players came up here — Jou-Jou, Silk, Spoon, Spice, Tiny . . ." Disco is feeling the rhythm now, talking and eating with gusto. "When Coney Island takes its game to other neighborhoods — Bed-Stuy, Red Hook, Brownsville — it's M-One. We ice 'em every time. Now it's getting out of hand. We always wanted other teams to fear us, but shit, now they see us coming and they give up. *They just walk away!*" Disco gestures grandly; Cheese Doodles fly across the court. "Now that's a damn shame," he says with real feeling. "Oh, well. What was I saying? Yeah, what you got to understand is, Coney Island never had big men. Most of our guys — Corey, Russell, Stephon — are guards. But we play fast and physical, and when you get hit, you don't cry. It's a pass-down thing: all the younger guys watch the older players and borrow from their game. And we got another ten years of great players on the way up, kids with an abundance of talent and that winning Coney Island attitude." Finished with his snack, Disco balls up the cellophane bag and cans it into an open trash barrel. His eyes light up with renewed fervor. "Damn," he cries, "I got a three-month-old son — he's already dunkin' Nerf balls!"

During the summer, Disco and Mr. Lou coach eight separate teams — 360 Coney Island kids in all — divided into three divisions: Bantams (ages fourteen and under), Juniors (fifteen to seventeen), and Seniors (eighteen to twenty-one). Practices are held at the Garden three times a week, on a mandatory basis. For years Disco and Mr. Lou worked exclusively with players from the six white brick buildings that make up the O'Dwyer Houses next to the Garden. Families in O'Dwyer, which have only eight apartments on each floor, tend for the most part to be small and stable, with at least one parent who works, and interested above all in keeping the peace in this relatively tranquil corner of the neighborhood. Tenant meetings at the O'Dwyer community center draw large, emotional crowds; and the project's kids go there to hang out, shoot pool, and watch college games on TV. O'Dwyer residents, knowing the resolve it takes to keep the more sordid aspects of the neighborhood at bay, have posted a sign in the doorway of the community center. "A MESSAGE TO DRUG DEALERS," it reads. "Stay out of public housing. We won't let you destroy our home and our kids. NEVER!!"

Eight blocks, but a world away, is the neighborhood's other large project, the huge mud-colored buildings of the Carey Gardens Houses. With up to fifteen apartments on each floor, Carey Gardens shelters many large, young, and often transient families on welfare. The chaotic conditions there, in which parents often move in and out leaving children to fend for themselves, have created fertile ground for the drug trade. Dealers enjoy hegemony of the project's dimly lit hallways and stairwells, and I have met Carey Gardens players who leave their apartments only for games, passing swiftly and with furtive looks through the project courtyard on their way to safer ground. Known as Drug Discount Land, the courtyard is a shadeless strip of walkways teeming with dealers, customers, and occasionally undercover cops, all maintaining a tense surveillance of one another.

For years, a deep hostility prevailed among O'Dwyer, Carey Gardens, and the other large projects in Coney Island. Dealers and players make up the principal social groups among young men in the neighborhood, and mimicking the territorial disputes of gang members, players from one block rarely spoke to those from another, and would never be caught at a rival project's court. But basketball helped to demilitarize the neighborhood. As the drug trade grew worse, distinctions of occupation — do you play or do you deal? — began to outweigh those of geography — are you from O'Dwyer or Carey Gardens? Suspiciously at first, players started meeting for games halfway between the projects in the neutral territory of Run-and-Gun Land. Then, several years ago, Mr. Lou started the O'Dwyer Tournament at the Garden, which quickly became Coney Island's premier competitive event. The tournament ran all summer, with each project fielding a "house crew," and for the first time Carey Gardens players would travel the eight blocks to compete with O'Dwyer kids on their home turf. Sensing a breakthrough in project relations, Disco and Mr. Lou then combined Coney Island's best players into an all-star team and took it to the city's other big tournaments: High Energy, Malcolm X, Soul-in-the-Hole, Citywide. "Now any one of my ballplayers can walk to another block and he'll find a fellow brother," Disco says. "Corey can dunk on someone down at Carey Gardens just like he can at the Garden — it's cool." (Corey, Russell, and Stephon all live in the Mermaid

Houses, which, in the neighborhood's social stratification, are considered safer than Carey Gardens but are not nearly as well kept as O'Dwyer.)

Few people who spend time with Disco and Mr. Lou don't at some point profess amazement at the program these coaches have assembled in this neglected neighborhood. At the start of one tournament game not long ago, a player dunked the ball and the ref's whistle fell right out of his mouth as he stared at the rim with his jaw gone slack. "Dunk that ball again," the ref said. The player did, and again the ref stared upward, incredulous that a neighborhood with gaping, unrepaired craters in the street would also have professional-style, spring-loaded rims that snap back after a player dunks. "You got *snap backs!*" the ref said. "In a *playground!*"

"Collegiate three thousands," Disco answered coolly.

"Ain't you worried someone's gonna rip them off?"

"Hell, no, this is Coney Island! And you'll notice" — here Disco abandoned his post on the sidelines and took the ref by the elbow, as though he would sell him the property — "this court is forty-six feet wide, just four feet narrower than the pros'." He looked at Mr. Lou. "How wide is West Fourth?" he asked, referring to the famous Greenwich Village playground.

Mr. Lou turned the question over in his mind. "Thirty, thirty-five feet," he said finally.

"There you go." Disco spread his hands wide, pleased by this new addition to his growing body of evidence.

•

Disco and Mr. Lou often speak with sorrow of other black, inner-city neighborhoods around the country, like the ones in Chicago, where drug dealers swagger up at neighborhood tournaments to recruit players straight off the court. Coney Island's devotion to basketball, they hope, will prevent that from happening here. "As long as we got the kids at the Garden, they're okay," Mr. Lou says.

But now that the camp season is over, and Russell, Corey, and the other players are all back in Coney Island, there's not much else to occupy them as the summer ebbs away, one infernally hot day after another, but to play basketball or sit around on the court benches sweating and talking about playing basketball. In past years, players often spent the last weeks of summer working at the local Burger King and Toys R Us. But few stores are hiring these days, and New York's fiscal problems have brought a suspension of most summer-job programs. Some Coney Islanders, knowing where they stand among New York's priorities, have begun joking mordantly that City Hall may soon shut off their streetlights to save electricity, and everyone will have to walk around the neighborhood with a candle.

And despite their athletic skills, and the crowds of coaches who watched them all summer, most of the players have returned to Coney Island completely broke and have found no legitimate options for making money besides hawking sodas on the boardwalk. It's hard work, lugging a case of Cokes from the nearest supermarket a mile away, then selling them one by one as the brutal summer sun hangs like a surgeon's lamp in the afternoon sky. For their trouble the players often get a summons from the police. Meanwhile, the drug business directly across Surf Avenue seems as brisk as ever and appears to draw less official attention. Later in the evenings, when the athletes start their workouts at the Garden, the dealers often gather at the sidelines to jeer — "You ain't goin' nowhere, *sucka!*" being one of their favorite taunts.

Normally the Coney Island tournament hits its stride in the last weeks of August, but this year's games are a meager reminder of better days. Even here at O'Dwyer there's too much drug dealing in the lot next to the Garden, and the players are wearying of the constant battles for turf. This year Disco can't even find any local stores to sponsor teams or help defray the cost of trophies and uniforms. "Remember when we used to have a thousand people come out to watch?" Disco muses. "We had to take down the fence 'cause people couldn't see? And we'd close off the street? Yeah, those games, those games . . ." I'm expecting Disco to launch into one of his prize monologues, but even he seems wrung out by the heat, and his voice drifts off.

On the walkway next to the Garden, a couple of college-age guys, one still in playing shape, the other going soft in the middle, walk by, kicking an empty beer can. When they played together at Lincoln a few years ago, everyone in Coney Island predicted they would be the ones to go all the way — maybe not the NBA, but at least the European league, where a first-year player takes home at least $75,000 a year. The thin one is now at his second junior college, still hoping a four-year school will sign him; he comes back to Coney Island in the summer to drive a cab and show off his playground moves at the Garden. The other one failed to graduate from Lincoln and has never left the neighborhood. Even with his current paunch, he's got an amazing game and comes out every afternoon to fool with the younger kids. But the air of lively expectation he used to wear like a plume is gone; he's given up. "Those were the guys who broke our hearts," Disco says.

I look to Mr. Lou, expecting him to temper his partner's remark, but he says, "It's true. They were probably the top two guards on the East Coast. I was very personally hurt that they never went anywhere. It was a real blow to the community." Everyone is silent with his own thoughts. A sea gull wheels in a great arc high above our heads, and from out in New York Harbor a fog horn groans, reminding me once again just where on the map we are. Then Mr. Lou, summoning his optimism, says, "We're hoping this new crew of players will be the ones who go to high Division-One schools. By the end of the summer, Russell's gonna have the complete package on the court and a damn near eighty average in school; he's the most impressive young man in the neighborhood. Corey should go D-One, too, if he'd just practice his goddamned outside shot. And Stephon — well, Stephon's got the whole package. If you say, 'Stephon, we need points,' no matter how big a guy is, you get points. If you need assists, you get assists."

Stephon Marbury, who will join Russell, Corey, and Tchaka on the Lincoln varsity when he arrives as a freshman next month, has been tearing up the camps this summer. I hadn't seen him play since that midnight game at the Garden, but I caught up with him one afternoon at the B/C camp in Pennsylvania, where administrators, following the rules and not their own eyes, had put him in with the fourteen-and-under group. Having played for years with his older friends at the Garden, Stephon was just toying with the youngsters in the junior division. All afternoon he would stand at the perimeter, doing a little stutter step — the top half of his body rocking forward while his feet stayed in place. When his defender backed off, Stephon dumped a three-pointer on him. When he was guarded tight, Stephon drove with ease to the basket. Soon his opponents were mobbing him with a double- and triple-team, but Stephon dribbled out of the thicket of limbs with a joyful expression and his gold chain doing loop-the-loops around his neck. Even the officials eventually got confused: Stephon has such a great handle, does so many tricks with the ball as he dribbles, that a couple of times the refs blew the whistle on him without actually knowing which rule he was supposed to have broken.

Stephon's advent at Lincoln next month may make the varsity squad the best it has ever been. Although Stephon is a freshman, he arrives with almost as much experience playing organized ball as Russell, Corey, and Tchaka. But looking back on the last few groups of neighborhood players, Disco and Mr. Lou are realizing that — notwithstanding all the promises made by the college coaches who visit the school each year to discuss scholarships and the route out of the ghetto — it's been years since a Lincoln player from Coney Island made 700 on his SATs, qualifying him to play Division I ball, and actually signed with a top school. Even the best Coney Island players, it seems, have been forced to enroll at two-year junior colleges, as the NCAA requires of players who don't make 700, before they can go on to Division I colleges. And few of those so-called juco players, now with only two years of eligibility remaining, were later recruited by four-year schools. Many Division I coaches refuse to recruit players once they enter the juco system, considering them damaged goods. So players who don't go directly from high school to a four-year college often never get to play top NCAA ball or earn their bachelor's degrees. Meanwhile, families who can afford the $2,500-a-year tuition at a Catholic school, or the Lincoln kids like Tchaka from neighborhoods better than Coney Island, seem to get their 700s and are recruited by all the Division I coaches.

As Disco and Mr. Lou tell it, the grim list of Coney Island players who fell short of their aspirations is growing all the time. In fact, the genealogy of Stephon's family, the Marburys, has begun to read like a cautionary tale of all the different ways a player's hopes can get dashed in this business: After starring at Lincoln five years ago, Eric (Spoon) Marbury, Stephon's oldest brother, was recruited by the University of Georgia, where he played alongside several future pros; but he failed to graduate before his scholarship ran out and has since returned to Brooklyn, where he works on a construction crew. Donnie (Sky) Marbury, the next son, displayed even greater promise in high school, but he didn't have a 70 average at Lincoln and had to do time at two junior colleges. After two years, he moved on to Texas A & M, where he led the Southwest Conference in scoring. But he never graduated either, and was passed over in the college draft. Now he's out in Utah, at yet another college, trying to finish his degree.

And then came Norman (Jou-Jou) Marbury. If ever Coney Island has produced pro material, it was he. The first public school player in New York to be named all-city three years in a row, Jou-Jou was a dazzler — fast, strong, with a deadly outside shot and the ability, on drives to the basket, to take on the largest foes. He had his pick of top programs and eventually signed with the University of Tennessee, which had assured him that if he chose their school, he could attend for free even if he didn't make 700 on the SATs; he would simply have to sit out his freshman season, as the NCAA rules require. But in the summer of 1990, just weeks before he was set to leave for Knoxville, Norman took the SATs one last time. His score improved by 90 points, but he still came up 40 points short of a 700. Tennessee broke its promise and withdrew its offer. Norman, Coney Island's finest product to date, packed his bags for a junior college in Florida. Since then he has played at junior colleges in Texas and Salt Lake City.

In the long line of stellar players who have come out of the Coney Island projects, Russell, Corey, and Stephon are considered the neighborhood's next great chance to reverse its fortunes. Given the earlier failures, however, these three players are being watched by Disco, Mr. Lou, and the rest of the neighborhood with a certain skittishness, a growing reluctance to care too deeply. Yet Coney Island does not offer its residents much else on which to hang their pride. So by unspoken agreement the misfortunes of bygone players are chalked up to a lack of will or to plain bad luck, either of which makes possible the continuance of hope. Silk Owens didn't go pro, it is said in Coney Island, "because that was the year they cut the college draft from three rounds to two." Others say his wife didn't want him to go pro. Another player, the explanation goes, had that pro game, went to the hoop both ways, "but he was done in by a shyster agent."

Still, the suspicion lingers that something larger and less comprehensible may be at work. Ten years ago the Long Island City projects in Queens produced New York's best players, until the drug industry and the collapse of that neighborhood into violence, broken families, and ever-deeper poverty put an end to its dynasty. In recent years the torch has been passed to Coney Island, which struggles to avoid a similar fate. "Something's wrong at Lincoln," says Mr. Lou. "Too many of our good ballplayers go to jucos. It's like a pattern."

"Yeah, and if they don't get this education thing fixed in the next two or three years, they'll get nobody from the neighborhood," adds Disco. "We hope this next group goes D-One, but if they don't, then forget it."

As Disco and Mr. Lou are talking, the heavy air collects around us with a menacing stillness. The sky, which had been neither cloudy nor clear, but bore the indistinct haziness of urban summer afternoons, turns the color of green bottle glass. Suddenly it begins to pour. We run into the O'Dwyer community center to wait it out. The center's day camp for toddlers is in session, and in the back some older guys are sitting at tables studying for their GED exams. The place is well scrubbed, conspicuously lacking in graffiti, even on the bathroom walls. The ceilings are low, supported by thick pillars, and the windows are covered with an intricate latticework of steel gates. Through the windows we watch the rain coming down in driving sheets, but we're snug in here, sealed off from the leaking ship.

Disco is sitting by the front door with some players, arguing about whether his Coney Island teams are, as he remembers it, undefeated over the last ten years for opening day tournament games. Karen Burton, who runs the community center and is known fondly among the players as Miss B, looks up from her desk and cries, "Basketball basketball basketball! All you guys ever talk about is basketball. All you guys ever do is play basketball. Do you ever wonder what it's like for the kids in Coney Island who *don't* play basketball? What are *they* supposed to do?"

Disco waves her away. "What do you mean, 'kids who don't play ball'! This is Coney Island. Everyone plays ball. Even my three-month-old is dunking Nerf balls." But his reprise of this line is sounded without its former vigor. "Basketball is all we got," he says more calmly. "There ain't nothing else to do in Coney Island."

"I know," says Miss B, turning back to her work. "That's exactly my point."

"You know, the YMCA on Surf Avenue was up for sale a while ago," Disco says. "The city could have bought that for the community but all they ever do for Coney Island is put up more rims. It's like they're trying to appease us." Miss B, flipping through papers on her desk, doesn't say anything but she's nodding. Outside, the rain stops as abruptly as it started, and we walk back over to the Garden. A few players try to disperse the puddles so that they can start a game. The air is just as hot and heavy as it was before.

Big-Time Recruiting

Six

"YOU HAVEN'T been up to see us? Here's a shot of our arena. Beautiful, isn't it? That's a ten-million-dollar building you're looking at. Every game sold out — a twenty-eight-thousand crowd. In four years you'll play in front of three-point-five million people. That's more than most pros! We're on TV more than any other Big East team. We play in Madison Square Garden four times a year. And we've been in the NCAA tournament for the last nine years in a row. Now you're gonna read in the papers about our kids getting benefits. But I want to assure you, our lawyers are working around the clock and they've found no major violations. The headlines say, PLAYERS GET CASH! Shit, I gave twenty dollars' Christmas money to one player. Big deal. Worst is, we'll lose a scholarship. But we won't be out of the NCAA tournament. Maybe we'll get a one-year probation during your freshman year, but we won't be out of the tournament. Okay, maybe — *maybe* — we won't play in the tournament, but that's it. Of course, I can't guarantee it . . . Anyway, have I mentioned the facilities? We got everything you want: great weight room, great student apartments, and we'll give you a meal card too — you can get pizza any time of the night. We got eleven thousand students. Fourteen hundred of them are black. Socially, nowhere better. Parties at night in the apartments. And our players — they should run for mayor! Always the most popular guys in town. Four sets of practice gear by Champion. And any model Nike you want. Any questions?"

Jim Boeheim, coach of the Syracuse Orangemen, pauses for breath. The sudden quiet is jarring, like the one that follows an insistent telephone cut off midring.

"Any questions?"

Tchaka, sitting across the table from Boeheim in the coaches' locker room at Lincoln High, remains silent. Arms folded in front of him, chin tucked into his chest, he watches Boeheim through his eyebrows — actually studies the coach's face — as though he might be called on someday to remember all its features for a police sketch. Ten days ago Tchaka finished his final summer camp appearance. This week he begins his senior year of high school. Already head coaches from Villanova, Seton Hall, Providence, Boston College, University of Miami, Florida State, Rutgers, Wichita State, and many other schools have requested audiences with Tchaka in order to convince him that his future will be best served by his spending the next four years in their company. The ones Tchaka has met with so far have offered him scholarships, extolled their athletic programs, hinted that they will make him a college star. But Tchaka, connoisseur of the game that he is, knows enough players who signed at top programs with similar dreams of making the pros — and then spent four years languishing on the bench — to believe that he now confronts, as the coaches often say, "one of life's no-lose propositions." No, from now until November 15, the earliest date on which high school seniors are allowed to sign with colleges, Tchaka must do what he does now: sit in this cramped, airless room and listen to the recruiters, hoping that his excellent radar will steer him toward those coaches he can trust with his future, away from those he should avoid.

"You know, Providence has got sophomores and juniors at your position. But a freshman's gonna play at Syracuse,"

Jim Boeheim is saying. "Normally it would be the other way around — you'd have to wait your turn at Syracuse. But with Billy Owens leaving early for the pros, we need another forward." The coach leans back in his chair and hooks his thumbs in his belt loops. He waits for Tchaka to ask a question, but none is forthcoming. "I think it's a great situation for you," Boeheim says, filling in the silence. "And the earlier you sign, the better."

A guaranteed starting postion in his freshman year — this is an unprecedented opportunity. And look where Owens is going: third pick in the college draft, soon to sign a contract worth $2.8 million a year with the Golden State Warriors. Tchaka has every Syracuse game from last season on tape. He has always admired the freedom they give their big men; Boeheim even let Owens, his power forward, dribble the ball upcourt on occasion. (Tchaka is a power forward.) But can Boeheim be believed? On the street, the coach has a reputation for "recruiting over" — that is, signing a player but giving his starting spot to a better athlete if one comes along. It is tempting for Tchaka to think Boeheim would never do that to *him*. Still, someone in this room runs a program currently under investigation by the NCAA, and it isn't Tchaka. Boeheim's thumbs are still hooked in his pants. The coach waits for some reaction from the recruit. Tchaka meets his gaze but says nothing.

•

The school year has begun without the usual, easygoing transition period that Lincoln's teachers and administrators always hope will linger at least through the first warm weeks of September. With summer still in the air, classroom doors are left open to cool down the rooms, and some students take full advantage — walking in and out of class, throwing projectiles through doorways at friends in the hall. One kid spends a large portion of his English class doing push-ups —

his legs in the hallway, his head bobbing up and down behind the back row of desks.

This year Lincoln will have eight security guards roaming the hallways with their walkie-talkies and a police officer patrolling the school entrance at dismissal time. One freshman wasted no time getting into the spirit of things; in the first week of school he punched the cop in the face. "Three arrests. Very auspicious," says one veteran teacher to his colleagues in the faculty cafeteria. Conversation there has already reverted to the usual topic — whether this year's kids are as bad as last year's or worse. "Remember the good old days?" says the vet. "When three student arrests wasn't considered a quiet day on the job? This is — what? — my eighteenth year at Lincoln? I must be an excitement junkie."

Lincoln's faculty does its best to maintain the academic standards of fifty years ago, when the school was considered a jewel in the Board of Education's crown and it graduated, among others, students like Joseph Heller, Arthur Miller, and three Nobel laureates in physics. In recent years, however, as the population of black and Hispanic students at Lincoln has grown past 50 percent, the school crossed the line that leads, in school districts everywhere, to white flight, reduced funding, lower SAT scores, and diminished faculty morale. At the same time, the city's beleaguered Board of Ed, desperate to keep the best students in the public school system, allowed the top Brooklyn high schools — Edward R. Murrow, Midwood, and Brooklyn Tech — to recruit the brightest kids from across the borough. The school-choice movement has put New York's public schools at war, and the traditional neighborhood schools like Lincoln, forced to accept all students who live within their zone, are losing the fight.

One day I took an informal hallway poll; I asked about twenty students where they had placed Lincoln on the list they were required to make as eighth-graders of the high schools they wished to attend. Lincoln never made it above fourth place; for most students, unable to secure a place anywhere else, it was the last choice. Just about the only students who enroll at Lincoln now as their predecessors once did — with the conviction that it will serve their future well — are its athletes. But as the list of Coney Island players who failed to qualify academically for Division I ball continues to grow, so too does the bitterness felt by many athletes and their families toward Lincoln High. This is the school, after all, to which Coney Island has always entrusted its finest talents, where a player is supposed to get his best shot at escaping the neighborhood. "Let's get this straight," Disco said to me a few weeks ago. "Lincoln didn't make Coney Island. Coney Island made Lincoln."

On the annual parent-faculty day in the fall, I finally met Russell's mother, Joyce Thomas. Tall and thin like her son, Mrs. Thomas seems to share all of Russell's extraordinary determination but not his debilitating self-doubt. From classroom to classroom she moved that day, meeting Russell's teachers and listening with a broad, proud smile as they praised her son for being one of the school's most dedicated students. After Mrs. Thomas was done, I offered her a lift back to her building in Coney Island. As we drove down Neptune Avenue toward the projects, each block more remote and less populated than the last, it occurred to me that Lincoln and its mostly white faculty offered Mrs. Thomas just about her only regular contact with the municipal powers that, through subsidized housing and other forms of public assistance, govern much of her family's life. If so, her experience with the school had not made her feel as though she and her family were enjoying the best the city had to offer. In my car, the polite demeanor with which she had greeted her son's teachers slipped away, revealing a startling candor. "Russell will make it through Lincoln. He will graduate. And he will go on to college. You can count on that," she declared, her resolute voice cutting through the sounds of traffic. "I am very proud of him for what he is doing. What child his age do you know is home by six, sits up every night at his kitchen table, and does his homework? What child his age do you know says, 'Ma, I got to go to sleep now, 'cause I got to get up soon and get myself to school'?" I could feel Mrs. Thomas watching me as I drove. Then she dropped her voice almost to a whisper, all the more commanding for its sudden hush. "You think it's easy raising three kids alone in a neighborhood like this? Well, it's *not*. Russell is helping me to show his two sisters the way out. But when it's their turn to go to high school, I will make sure they do just a little bit better than Lincoln. You understand me?" She paused and waited for me to nod. "Both of them have the ability to do a little bit better than *this*."

•

As Lincoln's academic program has worsened over the years, what little renown the school gets now comes almost exclusively from its athletic teams. Everyone at Lincoln seems to understand the dilemma, which is why — though administrators often bemoan Lincoln's reputation as the city's preeminent "jock school" — no one objects when, for example, funds earmarked for instructional repairs are diverted by the athletic department to fix backboards and football helmets. No one complains when a star athlete who scored 70 on a math test gets another 10 points on the house, as a helpful boost to his recruiting chances. And each September, when the college basketball coaches begin arriving — a parade of men in paisley and pinstripes, huge attaché cases, and gleaming gold NCAA rings — even the new principal comes down to the gym to soak in some of the glory. And this year's basketball players seem to be luring the most celebrated coaches ever — Jim Boeheim of Syracuse, P. J. Carlesimo of Seton Hall, Rollie Massimino of Villanova, and Rick Barnes of Providence, to name just a few. "Four Division One players in one year," Coach Hartstein keeps repeating. "That's got to be a record."

In Hartstein's locker right now, there are over 250 letters for Corey from midlevel Division I schools like Bowling Green, Rutgers, and Fordham. But Hartstein hasn't given them to Corey for the same reason that the college coaches, though they admire his stylish play, have held back from recruiting him: as his brother feared, Corey is spending too much time with girls, and his grades are still among the worst on the team. Stephon has just arrived as a freshman this month, and the coaches (some of whom have been sending him mail since he was in seventh grade) all ask Hartstein to introduce them to the Wunderkind. In fact, most of them would go ahead and dress the fourteen-year-old in a college uniform right now, but the NCAA might have a word or two to say about that. So the majority of coaches come, for the time being at least, to recruit Tchaka and Russell.

Most of them already know their way around the Lincoln corridors. As soon as Tchaka displayed glimpses of his potential last spring, Carlesimo, Massimino, and Barnes began dropping in on Coach Hartstein, just to tell him how much they liked Tchaka's game, to compliment Hartstein on his expert coaching skills, and to scan the school cafeteria for other men in suits. When they couldn't visit, they would write. Every afternoon now, Hartstein stops off at his school mailbox, filled with greetings from the coaches — one or two for Hartstein, dozens for Tchaka and his teammates.

Here's a note to Tchaka from the Providence assistant coach Fran Fraschilla, who sends along a snapshot of himself standing by the side of a lake holding up a fish: "Tchaka, growing up in Brooklyn, I never got a chance to fish much.

Last weekend, I got a chance to fish and it's a good thing that it's not my occupation because I'd be in trouble. Can't wait to see you! — Coach Fran."

An assistant coach from Fordham takes a more direct approach; he tells Tchaka about one scholarship recipient who became rich beyond his wildest dreams and later donated $10 million to the school. "Tchaka, this may be you someday. See how Fordham can change your life?" The coach ends his letter with the salutation "Health, Happine$$, and Hundred$."

Fraschilla touches base with Tchaka again, this time while on vacation in Florida: "Tchaka, I'm sitting here watching the Bulls and the Pistons on Sunday afternoon. You have at least one thing in common with them: *You play hard!* Hope you'll keep thinking about the Friars."

John Olive, an assistant coach at Villanova, drops Tchaka a postcard just to let him know that "I'm here with Charles Barkley at Villanova. Hope to talk to you sometime during the week. — Coach O."

And yet another postcard from the peripatetic Fraschilla ("just a note to say hello") while vacationing with his wife on some tropical island.

"Jesus, these guys could send Tchaka a scholarship just with their postal fees!" Hartstein grumbles. He reaches into his mailbox and disappears up to his shoulder. The letters come out in an endless stream, like a scarf from a magician's hat. "Here's one for a T-E-H-A-K-A Shipp," Hartstein notes wryly. A lot of coaches send form letters like this one to the Lincoln players. As Hartstein sees it, that's twenty-nine-cents' worth of interest — less, actually, since the schools mail in bulk. "The kid's got an unusual name. If they can't spell it properly, it doesn't show much interest, does it?" Hartstein rips that one up and tosses it into the trash.

The recruiting process inspires in Coach Hartstein both amusement and annoyance — the former because he watches up close the supplicating postures the coaches are willing to strike to woo his players; the latter because of the enormous time it requires on his part to monitor all the calls, visits, and mail. "If a college coach calls a player when I tell him not to," Hartstein says flatly, "then forget about recruiting that kid." But for all his protestations, lately Hartstein has not looked like a man who objects too strenuously to the attention his star athletes are bringing him. "He *says* he doesn't like the recruiting," Tchaka once remarked. "But I think he likes it more than me." That — and the complications it creates — became evident one afternoon in Albany last summer when a group of college coaches — Tom Sullivan from Seton Hall, John Olive from Villanova, and Steve Lappas from Manhattan College, a lower-level Division I school — invited Hartstein to join them for lunch at the local Ground Round.

The first half of the meal was devoted principally to shop talk: first a spirited debate over whether the three-point line in college should be moved back four feet in accordance with the pros; then a discussion of how the NBA has become so desperate to integrate its rosters that if you're tall and white and have the good sense to keep passing the ball to the black, $3 million-a-year superstar on your team, the front office will let you stay around the league for ten years; and finally a critique of the State University of New York at Albany, then hosting the Empire State Games. "What a waste of money to build such a huge campus," observed Sullivan. "Imagine the heating bills. And it's only Division Three!"

Hartstein was just beginning to enjoy this inside chat with the Big Boys. Then burgers and fries were delivered all around, and the coaches nudged the conversation toward more urgent matters. "You know, I think Tchaka could hold his own in the MAC division," offered Lappas, the Manhattan College coach.

Hartstein laughed and pushed back from the table slightly. "I knew there was a reason you were hanging out with a high school coach like me. You never do that except when you want one of my kids."

"Yeah, and how many of them have I gotten over the years?" replied Lappas.

"That's not my fault. I'm not telling Tchaka not to go to Manhattan," Hartstein said evenly. "In fact, I do more for you than I would for most coaches on your level."

"I tell you," Seton Hall's Sullivan interrupted, poking his head between the two, "if Tchaka winds up at Manhattan, there *will* be an investigation." This was meant as a joke, but no one at the table laughed.

"Seriously," Lappas went on, "Tchaka should come to Manhattan, 'cause he'll play thirty minutes a game there."

"Yeah, yeah," Hartstein replied with a smirk. "And if you were still an assistant at Villanova, and Tchaka was considering Manhattan, you'd say, 'What the hell does he want to go *there* for when he can go to Villanova?' You college coaches are all the same. You'll say whatever it takes to make your school sound better. And I understand that. That's your job." Hartstein shrugged. The conversation retreated to more neutral territory. When the waiter brought the bill, however, Hartstein pulled out his wallet, which prompted Lappas to nod in the direction of the Villanova and Seton Hall coaches. "With Tchaka on your team I'm surprised you don't have these guys buy you lunch," he quipped.

"If you weren't around," Hartstein shot back, "I'm sure they would."

Everyone laughed, but the meal concluded uncomfortably, leaving Hartstein stranded in that awkward zone, halfway between the kids he is obliged to protect and the coaches who bring him and his school whatever small degree of fame they enjoy.

•

"What's happening!" Rollie Massimino shakes Tchaka's hand and clasps his shoulder warmly. "How's your mamma? How 'bout school, kid?" In person, the Villanova coach is less imposing than he appears on TV; he is short and a bit round, with an ample jowl and thinning gray hair combed over a well-tanned scalp. He wears a dark pinstriped suit and huge gold wristwatch with a large *V* on the dial, and he carries a monogrammed briefcase. Immediately Massimino notices a small cut over Tchaka's right eye, suffered in a recent game, and he reaches up to inspect it with kindly, country-doctor hands. "You need to get that looked at," he says.

As he lays his case on the table, Massimino catches sight of a lush, four-color brochure from Seton Hall. As of last month, the NCAA banned colored recruiting brochures (along with, for certain arcane reasons, stationery printed in more than two colors and recruiting tapes longer than three minutes), and Massimino wonders aloud whether Seton Hall is distributing an old brochure to get around the rule. "That would be a good trick," he marvels, mostly to himself. Competition among college coaches may be fierce, but a shared contempt for the niggling NCAA rulebook always builds solidarity.

Massimino has arrived today with his son Tom, who is a Villanova assistant coach. As Tchaka, Coach Hartstein, and I take seats across from them, father and son click open their briefcases and remove six three-ring binders, each with a color-tabbed section: WHY THE BIG EAST, MEDIA AND TV, NCAA TOURNEY, and so on. Massimino arranges his fingers in a steeple, draws his breath, and begins the presentation in a rich, grandfatherly baritone. "In life, there's perception and there's reality, Tchaka. And believe it or not, life is more about perception. As a coach, I've been through it all — high school, small college, major college. So you can believe me when I say that the reality of Villanova is this: we're a family — very close, very selective. And I'm talking to you as a friend, telling you like it is, because I'm not a recruiter."

Massimino removes his reading glasses and, holding them by the stem, tries to lock eyes with Tchaka. "A lot of players want to come to Villanova — I don't need to tell you that. But we're only interested in a very few. When you come visit our campus, we ask the kids on the team what they think of you; no one else does this. And if our players don't like you, we won't recruit you. That's the truth. Why? Because we're a family, a family that wants happy people. That's one of my mottoes." Massimino returns his glasses to the bridge of his nose and lets his motto linger in the air.

Over the past few days, Tchaka has begun to notice a striking similarity among the coaches' maxims. "This is the second biggest decision you'll ever make — after you pick your wife" finds expression with some frequency, as does "Your next four years will dictate your next forty." But each coach sounds a slightly different theme, usually inspired by some bit of intelligence they have gathered about Tchaka — his home life, his buddies, whom he goes to for advice — anything to help the coaches make what they call "that essential emotional connection." One of the first details Massimino learned about Tchaka was how close the player had grown to his mother and sister in the years following the death of his father. Perhaps that is one reason the coach has arrived today with his own son.

"You want to go to a place that will give you the help, the guidance, the love," Massimino continues, with more vigor now, sculpting the air with his hands. "At Villanova, you'll come over to my house to eat. I'll even cook for you.

Because at Villanova, we play together, we eat together, we win together, we lose together, we cry together . . ."

On cue, Tom slides over to his father a three-ring notebook. "Here's something to show you the family component," Massimino offers. He turns to a page with mug shots of all the players he has coached since he arrived at Villanova in 1974, with a one-line description of each one's present occupation. The page heading reads: SEARCHING FOR YOUR POT OF GOLD. Massimino draws Tchaka's attention to a set of photos. "We have six brother combinations and one three-brother combo. No one in the country *ever* had three brothers on the same team!"

"True, true," Tchaka concurs. When Massimino first began talking, Tchaka was smiling and sitting, literally, at the edge of his seat, tipping it forward and balancing himself with both elbows on the table. Now he settles back and moves warily in his chair.

"What are the three things you look for in a college?" Massimino asks.

"Academics, athletics, and social life," Tchaka answers swiftly, having been asked this exact question twice by other coaches.

Massimino shoots his son a look. "Pretty perceptive kid, huh?" He turns back to Tchaka, places his hand over his heart, and declares, "I have never — not on my five children — asked that question that way and heard such a perceptive answer." He shuts the binder in front of him. "Tchaka, you are *the* perfect and ideal candidate for our program. I could have put away my books twenty minutes ago and said, 'That's it. There's no doubt.' And I don't say that a lot. Why do I say it now? It's the way you project yourself and exude your personality. It's because of what you can do — somebody a little bit bigger, a little bit better than the rest." Tchaka is now in full retreat — back tensed against his chair, arms crossed, chin tucked in.

Massimino leans toward the receding Tchaka and says, "Now we've got to talk about *when* you're going to sign. You're our number one guy, of course, but you should know that we're recruiting three or four other players at your position. As I say, if you sign with us early, it's all over. But I gotta tell you, the rest are ready to sign right now."

"What if I'm not?" Tchaka asks from his hideaway. Although the NCAA allows players to sign beginning on November 15, they can also wait for the so-called late signing period the following April if they want time to consider more schools.

"Look, ninety-five percent of the top players will sign early. That's just a fact."

"And if I want to wait?" Tchaka repeats with unexpected firmness.

Massimino seems taken aback by Tchaka's resolve. "So you'll sign next June, eh? With Hofstra? Or Queens?" His tone suggests that Tchaka might also take up girl's volleyball. "As I said, the other guys want in right now. So that's the chance you take. But" — Massimino draws his gold pen from his breast pocket and levels it at Tchaka — "if you want to pick your school instead of having the school pick you . . ."

"But all you coaches are looking to move," Hartstein suddenly interjects, with a small laugh. This is a daring remark, which explains the silence that follows it.

When a player signs a letter of intent to attend a certain school, the college's conference requires him to honor that commitment, whether or not the coach who recruited him stays around to honor *his* commitments. Now that many top coaches are compensated in the high six-figures (not to mention their million-dollar stipends from the sneaker companies), they regularly migrate from school to school, shopping for the best deal, unrestricted by the same rules that bind the players.

Massimino laughs lightly and says, "Twenty years ago, Tchaka, I could have promised you that if you came to Villanova, you and I would have a forty-year relationship. I'm older now, so I've got to say it'll be a twenty-year relationship. But ten years from now, you'll call me just to talk things over. Because if you don't" — Massimino points his pen at Tchaka with a severe expression, then lets his face break into a folksy grin — "I'll kick your ass!"

Tchaka's own smile arrives a second late, out of synch with the coach's quip, as he takes in Massimino's words. Among Tchaka's many talents, I have never observed one for clairvoyance. However, it is also a fact that were Tchaka to join the Villanova family next year, Massimino would be dispensing his help, guidance, and love three thousand miles away, to the players at the University of Nevada at Las Vegas.

•

After his session with Massimino, Tchaka leaves the locker room and runs into Russell, heading for his meeting with Rod Baker, the head coach at the University of California at Irvine. The two players have seen little of each other since the school year began, but the tension that marks their encounters arises right away. Trying to get past each other in the doorway, Tchaka and Russell move back and forth in perfect syncopation, blocking each other's path. Finally, Russell says, "So, you pass your SATs?"

"Yeah, I took them the day after the prom last June. Man, I was so tired the pencil kept slipping out of my hand." When Tchaka talks to Russell now, he sometimes looks past him into space. "You pass yours?"

"I got a six-ninety," Russell answers. "Only ten points to go."

"How 'bout Corey — he pass?"

"Nah, I don't think he's even taken them yet. He's relaxed about it, though. I'm relaxed about it, too," Russell adds, looking anything but. "Man, can you believe we're seniors already? High school is going by *fast!*"

"Not fast enough," Tchaka says. "Soon as I get to college, I ain't never gonna step in this school again."

Rod Baker comes around the corner. Russell and Tchaka back away from each other. Russell follows Coach Baker into the locker room.

•

"My apologies for not coming to see you before, Russell. It's not that we don't think you're a good player. It's just that ten days ago we didn't need you. But the fact is, one of our players just failed out and suddenly we need another guard." Coach Baker is a trim, handsome black man, one of the younger generation of Division I coaches coming to the helm at programs a step or two below the Big East. "And the first person we thought of was Russell Thomas. I'm not bullshitting you. Now, I know we're not a very good team at the moment. We won eleven last year, five the year before. But that's why we need guys like you. Frankly, I think you could be a pioneer at Cal-Irvine, an impact player, a franchise player. A year from now, when you're a freshman and we're playing for a conference championship, it won't take a brain surgeon to figure out it was Russell Thomas who got us there. And five years from now, I wouldn't be surprised if people are saying, 'Remember when Russell Thomas came in and completely changed the fortunes of Cal-Irvine?'" Baker runs a finger down each side of his well-groomed mustache. Russell smiles uncertainly.

"Cal-Irvine's old coach — he was successful, but his teams never guarded anyone. They gave up one hundred points eight times last year. The thing that excites me about you is that you can lock people up. Sure, you can bring the ball down and score, but you can also guard. One thing this team has never done is dig in its heels and say, 'You're not gonna score against us!' Sure, you're gonna have bad offensive games now and then, but you should never have a bad defensive game. It's gotta end, and it's going to end this year." As he listens to Coach Baker, Russell nods with every word.

"Now let me tell you about California. Ever been there?" Russell shakes his head. "Well, you're gonna think you died and went to heaven. I'm serious. What is it today — seventy degrees? Nice and sunny? In California this is a shitty day in December. That's the God's truth. Look at this guy." Baker gestures toward his white assistant coach, Greg Vetrone. "Just look at his tan. He's darker than *me!* When he opens his apartment door, he's ten feet from a pool!" Baker tosses his head back and laughs. Vetrone nods and says, "It's true."

"Now, Russell, of course you could go to a school like Rutgers. But consider the fact that they're only an hour away from Coney Island. The thing about going to school on the West Coast . . ." Baker looks down at his tasseled loafers, allows himself a moment to collect his thoughts, then looks up at Russell for his closing remarks. "In high school, Russell, you are a certain way either because you want to be, or because others see you that way. And sometimes you just can't get out of that. But everybody needs a fresh start sometimes. Everybody's got certain things they want to get away from in their past. In California, Russell, you can get away from that, from all the stuff that brings you down in Coney Island. At Cal-Irvine you can be whoever you really want to be . . ."

•

After the meeting with Coach Baker, Russell and I walk out to the football field behind Lincoln, a tree-lined expanse of green just a block in from Ocean Parkway, as lovely as it is incongruous in this otherwise barren setting. This is one of the first opportunities I have had to check in with Russell since the school year began, to see how he's coping with the recruiters. And it's a perfect day, too, one of those crystalline September afternoons, with fall in the air but the sun pulsing down on the aluminum bleachers where we sit with the last warmth of summer. (Weather like this may ruin Coach Baker's day out in California, but here in Brooklyn this is as good as it gets.)

Russell has honored that promise of his, made during the car ride back from the Empires, to assemble a new image for himself. On the first day of school this month he showed up amid the B-boy fashions of the Lincoln corridors wearing penny loafers, just like the college coaches. This little flourish excited about as much comment from Russell's friends as did his practice of shooting basketballs from a chair. But Russell, evidently as determined in fashion as he is in sports, forged ahead with his plan. The next day, building from the bottom up, he had added pleated pants . . . then a pair of suspenders . . . then a paisley tie. Finally, he topped off the look with a pair of nonprescription wire-rimmed glasses like the ones Tchaka occasionally wears — "because they make you look educated," he explained that day. "You know, the professor look."

Now on the bleachers Russell removes his glasses and polishes the lenses with his tie. "I was impressed with Coach Baker. I felt he was definitely leveling with me," he says. "But I'm going to wait and see. Hear what they all have to say. Then decide." He pauses and returns the glasses to the bridge of his nose. "Try not to be pressured, you know. Just take it one day at a time."

Although Tchaka is able to retain his poise with the coaches, asking questions and keeping his counsel, after a recruiting session is over it seems to take Russell a little while to locate his own thoughts. "They say it's the second biggest decision I gotta make in my life — after I pick my wife," he continues, looking around the field and swatting imaginary flies. "But I'm doing good, I'm handling it." He finds some gum on the bottom rung of the bleachers, picks it free, rolls it between two fingers, and flips it onto the grass. "It's normal to be confused, right?" Now he shifts his attention to the elastic of his right sock, performing a series of micro-adjustments to get the folds just right. "That's only human, isn't it?" Russell takes one more look around and, finding nothing else to distract him, falls silent.

Among the coaches recruiting Tchaka this month, many admiring words have been spoken about his strengths, both as a player and as a person. The coaches pursuing Russell seem to dwell on his presumed weaknesses. Like Rod Baker, several of the coaches have referred to Russell's incident on the roof last year, evidently hoping to suggest that even a high-strung kid like him will find a supportive, nurturing environment at their schools. The head coach from Saint Bonaventure, a small Catholic school in upstate New York, concluded his pitch by telling Russell, "You want to go to a school that's far enough away from home that you can re-create your personality, so anything you don't want people to know about you, they won't know." The coach from Wichita State built into his routine a little story about one of his players who lost his temper at a party, kicked in a door, and cut his leg to the tune of twenty-five stitches — the moral being not that you shouldn't kick in doors, but that "socially, it's not easy being a player." Fortunately, the coach was quick to add, the matter was settled without the filing of any charges.

Russell knows all too well his reputation as a "head case" and a player with "social problems," as Tchaka and some others are quick to say around Lincoln. And he is, undeniably, one tightly wound kid. But in some ways Russell's anxiety, which used to puzzle me no end, is beginning to seem a fitting response to the pressures of all the recruiting — by the summer camps and the scouting newsletters and the college coaches who show up at Lincoln, appraising, coaxing, negotiating, and, for all Russell knows, making promises they will never keep. It was, after all, Russell's fear of not getting recruited, as much as it was the actual fight with his girlfriend, that drove him to the edge of the roof that day.

In the popular imagination, being courted by all these college coaches is supposed to be a dangerously intoxicating experience. "Don't let it go to your head," everyone warned Russell before whispering cautionary tales about perks and promises, violations of NCAA rule, the lavishing of attention that turns poor ghetto kids into grasping pre-professionals. But in fact Russell finds little pleasure in being asked, at only eighteen years of age, to make the most important decision of his life, when he has nothing to fall back on if it doesn't work out right. Unlike Tchaka, Russell worries less about not getting good playing time in college than he does about finishing his college career with neither a degree nor any decent job prospects or, even worse, getting no scholarship offer at all — any of which would leave him like so many of his friends, stranded for the rest of his days in the Coney Island projects. And though Russell recognizes how fruitless it is to let his mind spiral into obsessive agonizing — which coaches are calling, which scholarship offers are genuine, which colleges will look after him properly when he gets to campus — now that the recruiters are here in the flesh, he seems more agitated than ever, restless with a set of emotions he can't even begin to identify.

"You know, I used to say that I couldn't wait to be a senior," Russell says to me now. "But to be honest, I got to worry about classes, the season, the newspapers, the recruiting." He shakes his head. "But my biggest concern is the

SATs. That's a lot of pressure." This year Russell continues his extraordinary study habits — skipping his lunch period to do his homework and carrying around his vocabulary flash cards wherever he goes. By dint of tremendous effort in class, he has brought his average up to 80, still the highest on the team. But he is, I can see now, fighting an uphill battle. Russell had trouble admitting it to Tchaka earlier today, but the first time he took the SATs he actually received not a 690, but a combined score somewhere in the mid–500s.

Getting a 700 — the eligibility requirement for Division I ball — did not strike me at first as a rigorous standard. But the national average for college-bound seniors, it turns out, is only about 800. And after becoming better acquainted with the quality of the Lincoln players' schooling and the environment in which they live, I am less surprised that they may not know a synonym for *panache* or how to make the most of what they do know; they've never been told, for example, to avoid guessing and answer only the questions they are sure of — the kind of test-taking tip suburban kids learn on their first day in a $600 Stanley Kaplan review course. Russell, after all, is struggling to answer reading-comprehension and algebra questions on the SATs when his schooling over the years has been so uniformly bad that he had never, until recently, finished a book or learned the fundamentals of multiplication. And the repeated frustrations of this test — the first of its kind he has ever taken in his life — are making him doubt the conviction that gave him such pleasure just a few months ago: namely, that he wasn't dumb; he just had never been properly taught how to learn. "How come it's always the guys who don't study who get their seven hundreds?" he says to me on the bleachers. "Tchaka and them guys sleep through the SATs and pass it, and seems like the guys who work hard always get screwed." He lets out a long sigh. "But, oh well."

The brilliant afternoon sun is still high in the sky, and from across the football field the chants and cries of cheerleading practice travel toward us with perfect clarity, as if over open water. Russell shades his eyes with his hands and watches a tumble of cartwheels. "It's nice out here, isn't it?" he says. "All the trees and everything? Out where I live there's nothing but total corruption and evilness, drugs and stolen cars. All my friends be selling drugs, getting arrested, shot at. In Coney Island, man, someone dies, it's like 'So what?'" Russell watches the cheerleaders with a vacant look. Then he says, "You heard what happened to Chocolate, right?"

I have. Of all the great Coney Island players whom basketball failed to deliver to a better life, David (Chocolate) Harris suffered the cruelest end. Chocolate was a teammate of Russell and Corey's, but he dropped out of Lincoln a few years ago and fell under the sway of the neighborhood's gang culture, eventually becoming a small-time drug dealer himself. Last summer the police found him in an abandoned lot, his sweatshirt hood pulled over his head and a bullet hole in his skull. He was seventeen years old. Some of his friends and former teammates memorialized him by writing, on the tongues of their sneakers, CHOCOLATE: R.I.P.

"No one really knows how Chocolate died, you know," Russell says. His voice has no volume. "I heard like three different stories — that his girlfriend's old boyfriend shot him. Then I heard that he tried to rob someone and they pulled a gun. And then I heard that it was one of his friends shot him. But as soon as the cops found out he was a dealer, they just closed the book." Russell is still looking off into the distance. "Things happen so fast. Man, life goes by so fast."

Once again Russell starts to busy himself, this time by rearranging the gear in his gym bag: sneakers, towel, basketball. Something bothers him, though, and he keeps going back to it, searchingly, like a tongue to a broken tooth. "You know, I look at all these players from Coney Island, like Silk and Jou-Jou. They're *way* better than me, and look what happened to them. Jou-Jou lost his scholarship to Tennessee when he didn't pass his SATs; Silk never graduated from Rhode Island . . ." Russell runs his hand over his scalp. "This recruiting business, man, it's scary — something always messes you up. But Coach Baker," he adds, "for some reason he made me feel comfortable and secure, like he'll take good care of me, like I'm part of the family."

During the time I've spent with Russell so far, he has almost never mentioned his own family. Even after my car ride with his mother I know very little about his home life, only that his father, a construction worker, moved away when Russell was extremely young, leaving his mother to raise him and his two younger sisters. It's only speculation, of course, but I can't help wondering if it isn't even more difficult for Russell to resist the high-powered coaches who are recruiting him this month because he has lived most of his life without a father and, at the same time, has sought desperately to avoid the pattern set by almost all the other grown men in his neighborhood, except perhaps for Willie Johnson, Disco, and Mr. Lou.

Just at that moment Russell's new girlfriend, Terry, comes into view across the football field. She waves to us and starts walking toward the bleachers. "Now that girl is *smart!*" Russell exclaims. "She got an eighty-eight average in school — she makes me look bad!" A cloud has just shifted in Russell's mood and the sun has reappeared. "She got a *nice* family too. Her mother's a teacher. Her father's a principal. One of her aunts is a *nun!* They even got their own house, over in Flatbush." Terry is the first woman Russell has been serious about since his fight with his old girlfriend last year, and the two have been inseparable from their first date together, going to movies and picnics and romantic strolls along the boardwalk. Every time Russell is delayed at practice, he dispatches one of the varsity managers to locate Terry and insist that she wait for him. Given the disappointments over fellow players like Silk and Jou-Jou, and the deaths of friends like Chocolate, it must come as a great relief for Russell to have found someone from a stable family and a relatively safe neighborhood (the Flatbush section of Brooklyn is one of the borough's few decent black middle-class areas), not to mention someone as pretty and levelheaded as Terry.

On the whole, Russell's friends are thrilled to see him involved with her, noticing right away the calming effect she seems to have on him. Terry's friends wonder whether she's lost her mind. But despite their warnings, Terry has stuck by Russell, accepting the ring he gave her not long ago as a token of his affection, even helping him with his schoolwork. And recently Russell announced to his teammates that he would wear a small pink patch (Terry's favorite color) on his uniform this season. "People say we're young, it can't be that serious. But I love Terry, I really do," Russell says, zipping up his gym bag. "She's a junior, you know, so after I leave for college next year she'll still have another year at Lincoln. But she won't see nobody here when I'm gone. I really think in my heart that Terry and me will end up together. Like two birds who fly apart and somehow, many months later, fly back together again." Russell smiles, and the expression looks foreign on a face so often lined with worry. "A girl like Terry don't come along every day, you know," he says, giving me a little nudge in the ribs. "One of these days, I'm gonna marry that girl."

Terry is still a good fifty yards away. Suddenly Russell puts his hand on my arm. "You know what happened to me last year, with that business on the roof?" he says. This is the first time Russell himself has mentioned the incident to me; perhaps the comforting sight of Terry's approach has given him the presence to bring it up. "I really thought my career was shattered when that happened. People were always saying, 'Yo, you better watch out, or Russell's gonna start acting crazy again!' But you know, I see now it was good for me." He nods. "I been through certain things other teenagers haven't. I learned that part of success is failure, having hard times smack you in the face, having to go without having." Still gripping my arm, Russell looks me in the eye and says, "I'm gonna get my seven hundred and go Division One. Trust me. You know why?"

"Why?"

"Because I've come too far, worked too hard already."

Terry is almost upon us now. Russell licks his fingertips and cleans a smudge off the top of his loafer. "Nothing's gonna stop me," he says, still smiling and rising to his feet. "Nothing." Then he takes a precautionary, pre-date whiff of each armpit and, finding the results tolerable, shakes my hand and runs off to meet his girl.

Seven

RICK BARNES does not have a monogrammed briefcase like the other college coaches. He does, however, have a deck of cards. Standing in front of Tchaka, the Providence coach riffles the deck one way — looks like the usual fifty-two. Then he riffles it the other way — hey, they're all the two of spades! With a flourish, Barnes places a ball of paper under one of three cups, mixes up the cups, then asks Tchaka to guess which cup covers the ball. There it is — gone! And what is this? A quarter hiding behind Tchaka's ear!

If Massimino & Son presented themselves like estate lawyers promising Tchaka a share of the family fortune, Barnes, standing in the coaches' locker room at Lincoln High, looks like some sort of graduate-student magic act. He is a good-looking man in his late thirties, with a soft Southern accent and sparkling blue eyes. From head to toe he is freshly pressed, not a wrinkle in sight, except maybe near the eyes, which turn down at the corners and give him an expression of perpetual merriment. Apparently card tricks are not the only thing he has up his sleeve. As all of us — Barnes, his assistant Fran Fraschilla, Tchaka, Coach Hartstein, and I — take seats around the table, Barnes looks at me and says, "So. You've been sitting in on all these recruiting meetings, haven't you? What have you learned so far?"

What?

"Go on. Why don't you show us what you've learned? *You* play the college recruiter. I'll watch. What are you going to say to Tchaka?"

Well, this is a novel strategy. Quite the way to charm Tchaka. And, given how many coaches have preceded Barnes, a shrewd way indeed for the Providence coach to separate himself from the pack, to show Tchaka how absurd he considers all this recruiting, even as he goes ahead and recruits the player. However, there must be some way for me to avoid this. I look at Tchaka. Will he toss me a life preserver? No, he's already turned his chair in my direction, grinning expectantly. The NCAA, perhaps? They've got rules for everything; surely one exists to prohibit role-playing during the recruiting process. But the time for stalling is up. I must begin.

I tell Tchaka that he's a young man with great prospects. I predict that with him — and I don't say this to everyone — the sky will truly be the limit. But he needs to go to a place that will help him actualize his potential, because the next four years of his life may dictate the next forty. "Now I'm not going to promise you a starting position, Tchaka, but I *am* going to promise you the chance to earn it. Because that's what this game is all about — working hard, achieving results, making yourself the very best basketball player you can be. Because a person can overcome any obstacles if they want it enough . . ."

I've got the music going nicely — Tchaka and I are beginning to waltz to the melody of my sweet, empty promises — when Barnes casually elbows me aside and starts dancing with Tchaka himself. "He's kidding about it, but what he says is absolutely true," the coach begins. "This game *is* about hard work. And if you don't want to work hard, don't come to Providence, Tchaka. I'm serious. If it means me being tough, I'll be tough. Hard work is the only way to win." Barnes is stepping lively now; Tchaka has awarded him his complete attention, and I'm back where I belong, watching the couple from the edge of the dance floor. "For instance, we make our players get up for breakfast at eight o'clock," Barnes continues, "even if their first class isn't until ten-thirty. Because I don't like guys running out the door at ten-twenty with their shirts unbuttoned and looking like a mess. Impressions are important. That's why I want you. You work hard. You play hard."

With that, Barnes twirls Tchaka into the arms of his assistant coach. "You know, Tchaka, in Rick's first year as head coach of the Friars, Providence was picked to finish ninth in the Big East," says Fraschilla. "Well, the Friars went out and won their first thirteen straight, and they went into the NCAA tourney. We fear nobody. Rick's attitude is: we'll play anybody, anytime."

So this is Providence's theme: The Little Engine That Could. Tchaka wasn't a born star, but he made himself into an all-American; Providence may be a Big East underdog, but they'll fight to the bitter end. "That's right. I don't care if I sign Shaquille O'Neal," declares Barnes. Hearing this, Tchaka allows his right eyebrow a slight elevation. He knows that Barnes would drop to his knees for O'Neal, the LSU star and future NBA sensation. "I'm serious. I'd rather have Marques Bragg," Barnes says of the journeyman Providence player. "Maybe I'd find a spot for Shaquille, but he's not gonna take Marques's position. Our hard workers, they're the heart and soul of the team." Barnes makes a pistol with each hand. "There's a player who plays with Michael Jordan by the name of Scottie Pippen. He didn't have exposure in college, he didn't play on TV. But" — Barnes aims both barrels at Tchaka — "he's great because his heart is bigger than his chest. And you're that kind of player too."

"It's true," adds Fraschilla. "If one guy we saw last summer epitomizes what Coach Barnes stands for — you know, blue collar, work ethic — it's you."

This is not precisely the music to which Tchaka's heart quickens. Praising him for his proletarian play — by which the coaches usually mean hustling for rebounds and diving for loose balls — is like commending an aspiring slugger for his peerless sacrifice bunts.

"I don't know if you'll be a shooter, Tchaka," Barnes says, losing the rhythm now. "I can't promise you that. But I like you because you play hard. That's your best talent. And I won't promise you you'll start either, but I give you my word: I'll give you the chance, and if you get it, it'll be because you earned it."

This seems only to confirm Tchaka's darkest suspicions — that Barnes was planning to use him as a role player, the one who would come off the bench when the stars needed a rest.

"Are you recruiting anyone else at Tchaka's position?" Coach Hartstein asks, on behalf of his player.

"Just him," says Barnes.

"Just him?" Hartstein repeats.

"And John Wallace, but he's a perimeter player."

"That's it?"

"Well, we're looking at Robert Blackwell too."

"Anyone else?"

"No, that's it."

Fraschilla leans forward with one final thought. "We might not be ready to contend for a national championship this year or next," he says, "but by your junior and senior years, Tchaka, we'll have it all in place. And I know I sound like a preacher, but I get fired up because I believe in what Coach Barnes is doing. You see, we're in this for the long haul." (Long haul, short haul — everything is relative. By next season Fraschilla will have abandoned his Providence post for the head coaching job at Manhattan College.)

Finished with their presentation, Barnes and Fraschilla rise to their feet. Then Barnes pulls from his bag a custom-designed recruiting booklet and presents it to Tchaka. Looking down at the cover, Tchaka sees his own picture under the title: AN ALL AMERICAN BOY. Inside it reads, "Ray Flynn . . . Lenny Wilkens . . . Marques Bragg . . . John Thompson . . . Tchaka Shipp . . . The tradition continues!" Tchaka grins but inspects the booklet like a store clerk examining a questionable fifty-dollar bill; he all but holds it up to the light.

Pleased with how his pitch seems to have gone, Barnes smiles and runs two fingers down the front of his burgundy silk tie. He gathers his recruiting materials and shakes hands all around. Almost as an afterthought, he reaches into his breast pocket for his deck of cards — there's still time for one more trick. When Barnes pulls out the deck, though, he loses his grip, and all fifty-two cards scatter across the floor. Tchaka peers over the table before Barnes can scoop them up, and sees that each trick card has been stamped with a two of spades. He starts laughing, quietly at first, then with mounting giddiness — happy to have made it through yet another presentation, delighted as well to have caught Barnes at his own game. Tchaka winks at me so that I can enjoy the moment too. But my mind is focused on the events of a half-hour ago, trying to determine how I got pulled so easily into Barnes's little game, and wondering why I have this peculiar aftertaste from having been cast as a college recruiter for the day.

•

"Come on, Russell — we're jetting!" Stephon places his hand against the back of Russell's bald head and flicks it hard to make the skin sting.

"Damn, Stephon, stop sweating me!" Russell cries, his voice high and strangulated. "Can't you see I'm talking to my girl?"

"*Can't you see I'm talking to my girl?*" Stephon mimics.

Russell tries to ignore him. He whispers in Terry's ear, gives her a kiss, slings his book bag over his shoulder, and marches toward the locker room. The last class bell has rung, bringing rush-hour congestion to the Lincoln corridors. Stephon lingers in the crowd and leans in close to Terry. "You know, when Russell goes to college, I'm next in line."

Terry is almost as tall as Stephon, and for an instant I think she's going to hit him. But she says, "You got *some* mouth," and simply walks away.

Stephon does not suffer from the usual array of adolescent insecurities, but there's no reason that he should, given that his arrival at Lincoln last month as the fourth — and arguably most talented Marbury boy — was anticipated throughout the school as if he were Magic Johnson returning from retirement. All the seniors have been awaiting Stephon's advent at point guard, where, it is hoped, he will flawlessly deliver the ball into their hands for easy baskets. And Bobby Hartstein, who usually gives incoming freshmen a grudging nod at best, has allowed Stephon his choice of team jerseys and has even given the first-year player the combination to his own locker so that Stephon can store his schoolbooks there during practice. Stephon has not exactly been immune to all the hype. In the first week of school, he asked one of his classmates to carry his books; a few days later, a girl in the corridor asked if he was *the* Stephon Marbury and he replied, "Yeah, but I don't know *you* from a can of paint." And Stephon's profile will in no way diminish when he takes the court this afternoon during the season's first official varsity practice. Hopes for this year's team are running so high around school that a small crowd begins to gather in the gym: students, teachers, other coaches, even a reporter for *Newsday* who will cover the team almost daily this season.

The players do not disappoint. Corey arrives for practice a few minutes late, but once he's on the court (wearing a pair of checkered pastel Bermuda shorts), he makes up for lost time — blowing past everyone who tries to guard him, making acrobatic excursions to the hoop, and playfully slapping his opponents' heads as he goes in for the dunk.

Tchaka, looming above everyone, completely dominates both ends of the court — blocking shots, rebounding, tipping in missed attempts — in essence demanding a cut on all transactions within a three-foot radius of each basket.

As for Russell, he is no longer just a stationary jump shooter, as he was during the summer-camp season. Having worked much of August with Mr. Lou, he is now shooting off the dribble and taking it to the hoop with surprising authority. At one point during today's practice, Russell drives the lane and goes straight over Corey for an emphatic jam. The whole place goes wild — everybody in the gym is chanting Russell's name; guys are yelling, "He flushed it *good! He threw* it on him!" Russell, ignoring the cheers as always, walks over to me and squeezes my shoulder with a serious grip. "See, I told you I would wear nice shoes this year, and I did. I told you I would dunk, and I just did. It's all part of the plan."

Hmm.

And then there is Stephon. He is making his official debut as a high school player today, but he takes the court as he always does — confident, leaning forward on the balls of his feet in happy anticipation, arms jangling at his sides. "Mission day," he announces with a clap. "Time to get busy." Within moments he is making quick work of his older competition, stunning the crowded, noisy gym into a reverential silence. Here he is, out by the three-point line. He does a stutter step to freeze the defense, then drives the lane. In midair, he encounters Tchaka's six-foot-seven-inch presence, so he changes direction, shifts the ball from right hand to left, and sinks a reverse lay-up. Coach Hartstein, getting his first look of the season at Stephon, mutters,

"Holy shi—," not even finishing the thought, because here Stephon is again, off to the left. He drives, sees too many bodies in the paint, and pulls up for a jumper. He is way out of position, his lithe body still floating toward the basket, so he calculates his velocity, takes a little something off the ball, and banks it gently off the glass.

It's not just that Stephon is a great young player; he does things you simply cannot teach in this game. As point guard, setting up plays for his teammates, Stephon always keeps his head up and sees the court as if he had one eye in the usual spot and the other near the ceiling, looking down. He goes up for a jumper and, eyes fixed like radar on the rim, guns the ball inside to a surprised Russell for an easy lay-up. *How could he have seen that?* Running the fast break with Corey, he picks up his dribble, cradles the ball in the crook of his arm, and whips a diagonal bounce pass through two defenders as effortlessly as if he were lazing by the shore, skipping stones. ("Deliver the pizza, cuz, *with* pepperoni!" Corey cries on his way to the hoop.) This sort of command one sees only among genuine child prodigies — Itzhak Perlman playing Paganini at the age of five — the ability to perform the easy and difficult passages with the same fluid grace.

Stephon began his study of the game at approximately three years of age. At six, he could shoot and dribble with both hands; a few years later he would show up at halftime during Lincoln games, steal the ball from the ref, and begin tossing in three-pointers with such pinpoint accuracy ("bye-bye birdie," he would chirp) that the net gave but the slightest shiver. When he reached the advanced age of ten, Disco and Mr. Lou let him captain one of their fourteen-and-under teams. The next year, Stephon scored an astonishing 41 points in a Catholic Youth League championship game, making the *New York Daily News* for the first of what would turn out to be countless occasions. Even as an eighth-grader,

Stephon still looked unimposing — just a scrawny kid whose narrow shoulders could barely support his tank top — and he spent most of his nonplaying time worrying that he'd never grow tall enough to dunk. But his advanced skills and size eleven-and-a-half feet gave an auspicious picture of what he'd be like full grown and strong enough to wreak complete havoc on the court.

•

That college coaches like Boeheim, Massimino, and Barnes would consider no entreaty beneath them in their pursuit of a high school senior like Tchaka was apparent to me by now. What I hadn't known until Stephon joined his older friends on the Lincoln varsity is that the feverish recruiting of top players actually begins when they are fourteen and in junior high. Stephon may have grown up in one of the city's most isolated communities, but by the time he was ready to pick a high school last spring, everyone associated with prep basketball throughout the five boroughs had heard of him, and every school within a thirty-mile radius of Coney Island began its recruiting. Catholic schools like Bishop Ford, Tolentine, Bishop Loughlin, Christ the King, Saint Raymond's, and Xaverian placed their bids — promises of a starting position from some schools, a guaranteed supply of his favorite sneakers from others. One Brooklyn coach presented Stephon with a new uniform and treated him and his father to a series of extravagant dinners. A coach in the Bronx was rumored to have offered cash up front.

And the recruiters arrived not only from the big-time parochial schools. Technically, of course, kids in the New York City public school system must go to their neighborhood zoned schools. But when it comes to talented athletes like Stephon, the PSAL finds so many loopholes in the admissions procedures that public school coaches have begun recruiting eighth-graders the same way the college coaches go after the seniors — by promising them the most playing time, the best chance to win a city title, and the exposure to get recruited to the next level. ("They've been after me since I was in fifth grade actually," Stephon once told me.) The PSAL is now riddled with players crisscrossing the city to play on their favorite teams, others whose grades (and second-grade reading levels) should have rendered them ineligible, as well as nineteen- and twenty-year-old kids who shouldn't even be in school. One graduating senior, having failed to sign with a good college, managed to get himself reclassified as a high school junior because of poor eyesight, though it didn't seem to hurt his shooting touch.

Since most of the Coney Island projects fall within its school zone, Lincoln automatically gets a new crop of exceptional athletes every year, which saves Coach Hartstein the trouble of scouring all of Brooklyn's junior highs for the next great class of players, as certain coaches are known to do. But to maintain its hegemony in the PSAL, Lincoln does have to prevent other high schools from poaching on its turf. Directly across Ocean Parkway from Lincoln, for example, sits William Grady, another powerhouse PSAL team and Lincoln's chief rival for the pool of talent coming out of the Coney Island projects. Both Lincoln and Grady enlist the aid of coaches and teachers at the so-called feeder schools — the grammar and junior high schools through which the neighborhood kids must pass — in order to steer the best players to their schools.

Hanging out at the Garden last summer with Disco and Mr. Lou, I also discovered that both Lincoln and Grady send unofficial representatives into the neighborhood to troll for players, just as the college coaches do. Grady's recruiter is Derrick (Jock) McMahon, a tall, heavyset black man who lingers around the Coney Island courts warning kids that if they go to Lincoln, they'll never score 700 on their SATs and make it to a Division I school. Like the college recruiters, Jock does not easily part with the animus he feels toward those kids who chose the competition. When Jock ran into Tchaka at a camp last summer, he stood there scrutinizing the player with his arms folded across his chest. "You may have played at Nike," Jock told him, "but you're still corny" — that being the latest term on the street for hopelessly uncool. "I don't know why you even play. You're never gonna get the ball." ("Guys like Jock are why I can't wait to get out of New York," Tchaka remarked later. "He's the type of guy who says, 'You're not going anywhere.' Then he sees you on TV and says, 'Hey, I know him!'") Lincoln's principal recruiter is the varsity trainer, Tony Grittani, an affable man who can always be counted on to have a few treats — free tickets to Lincoln basketball games and such — to hand out to the neighborhood players. It was Grittani who, three years earlier, spotted Russell playing at the Garden and persuaded him to enroll at Lincoln.

Grady, which is a vocational school, can legitimately enroll players from anywhere in New York City as long as they attend in order to take technical classes not offered at other schools. One does begin to wonder, though, when kids who have spent three years at an academic high school get into an argument with their basketball coach and abruptly transfer to Grady, avowing a sudden passion for the organized study of automotive repair. Enrolling players from outside the neighborhood is considerably more difficult for a zoned school like Lincoln, although ways have been devised there too. In recent years, Lincoln has established two special "magnet" programs — Pre-veterinarian Animal Science and the Institute for Professions in the Sciences — in order to compete with Midwood, Murrow, and Brooklyn Tech for the borough's brightest students. The programs are also used to bring in kids with an aptitude for slam-dunking a basketball. Tchaka, for example, then living in Bed-Stuy, was brought onto the Lincoln varsity by Grittani, the school's transfers-and-eligibility wizard, who walked him through the admissions procedures as an out-of-district student in animal science.

Perhaps the most cut-throat recruiting on any level — high school or college — actually goes on in the summer leagues among the privately sponsored basketball clubs, the highest profile of which are the South Bronx Gauchos and the team affiliated with the Riverside Church in Manhattan. Bestowing on its mostly impoverished players the official and highly coveted Gauchos jackets, shorts, and athletic bags, Gauchos' coaches select upwards of five hundred kids, ages four to nineteen, warehousing them into a farm-league system of teams (Pee Wees, Biddies, Midgets, Juniors, and Seniors) that will keep the organization flush with talent for years. Like recruiters on every level, summer-league coaches talk endlessly about "doing it for the kids," about how "academics comes first around here," about how the bond they form with their players lasts for years. "They know I'm not out to steer them the wrong way or for personal gain," one coach said to me — an odd remark indeed, since we were talking at the time about something I assumed to be completely unrelated: why inner-city kids seem to prefer Nike over other sneaker brands. But just as the thief will inexplicably return to the scene of the crime, the summer coaches can't stop themselves from raising the issue of self-interest. For they too receive stipends from Nike in exchange for keeping their players wearing the famous swoosh; and they too are courted by the top college coaches, who never lose sight of the ways a summer-league coach may influence which college one of his players will ultimately attend. Perhaps more than anyone else in this business, the summer coaches ride on the coattails of the city's great players, forming their résumés by "how many pros I've produced over the years," as one coach said to me in a rare moment of candor.

The rivalry between Lincoln and Grady is nothing compared with the ill will generated in the summer leagues, where coaches sometimes refuse to shake each other's hands at tournaments and spare absolutely no expense to win. Last summer one team, after losing two games in a Las Vegas tournament, flew in ringers from New York City. And according to one coach, summer-league teams will even raid each other's stars with under-the-table payments — $250 for a regular game, $500 for a tournament — which is no small inducement to indigent ghetto kids.

During the summer season, Tchaka and Corey both avoid the Gauchos and the Riverside Church, preferring the low-key style of the Madison Square Boys Club in Manhattan. (While other teams fly to out-of-state tournaments, the Boys Club coach, Doc Nicelli, loads everyone into his van and takes rural routes the whole way to avoid the highway tolls.) Russell, of course, shuns the summer leagues altogether, preferring his solitary workouts at the Garden. Stephon, however, is a new breed of Lincoln player: he plays with Riverside *and* the Gauchos. "You go both ways, is that it?" Hartstein said to him one day. "Whoever gives you the most?"

"You got it," Stephon replied.

To his credit, Coach Hartstein tries to keep his distance from this feeding frenzy and to resist the pressure that builds, even on high school coaches, to assemble a winning program at all costs. ("You always hear people complaining about what big heads these kids have," he observed, rather pointedly, while lunching with the college coaches in Albany last summer. "Well, who gave it to them?") Considering himself as much a teacher as a coach, Hartstein prefers to work with any player who happens to walk through the door at Lincoln. When Stephon was in the process of narrowing his choices for a high school last spring, Hartstein assiduously kept a low profile and hoped that Lincoln would have the edge simply because Stephon's older brothers — Eric, Donnie, and Norman — had starred at the school and older friends of Stephon's, like Russell and Corey, were already there.

But something about Stephon's amazing repertoire of skills seems to soften the resolve of even the highest-minded coaches; and Hartstein, it must be said, could not resist making a few subtle advances toward the young player. Though he normally forbids most Lincoln students from watching varsity practice (including the sports reporter for the student newspaper), for the last three years Hartstein welcomed Stephon into the gym with a big hug. And when the team played for the city championship at Madison Square Garden last spring, Hartstein reserved an honorary place for his incoming star on the Lincoln bench. For a time, toward the end of last summer, it looked as though Stephon might go into the Catholic league after all. Stephon had grown wary of Lincoln after two of his brothers, Donnie and Norman, failed to meet the minimum NCAA academic requirements and were forced to attend junior colleges. Vowing not to go that route, Stephon thought he might get better academic preparation at a Catholic school. But then Hartstein made Stephon an offer that would be considered extraordinary in almost any business but this: the forty-two-year-old coach promised the fourteen-year-old player that he'd turn down any college coaching offer over the next four years so that he could personally shepherd Stephon through high school.

And Hartstein has wasted no time honoring his promise. Ever since the school year began, he has had a private word with Stephon at the end of nearly every day. Other teachers have watched these hallway conferences with a certain distress. As rigorous as he is with most of his players, disciplining them in practice and helping them with their schoolwork, Hartstein has always found it difficult to hold the talented Marbury boys to the same high standard. Stephon's three older brothers each received preferential treatment: academic courses were dropped for things like fashion design, according to several teachers; excuses were made for cut classes and rowdy behavior. Now it looked as if the coddling was starting all over again. The season hadn't even begun, and already Hartstein was cornering Stephon's teachers in the hallways to lobby on his behalf and giving his star player awkward little hugs and the key to the teachers' bathroom. One day, in order to compete with the generosity of the summer coaches, Hartstein asked Stephon whether he would like free tickets to a Seton Hall game. "If you ever want to go, let me know," Hartstein told Stephon. "I know P. J. Carlesimo very well." Seeing the look of interest that crossed Stephon's face, Hartstein added quickly, "I know Rick Barnes and Rollie Massimino very well too."

So when Stephon concludes his stunning performance during the season's first practice with a three-pointer off the dribble, wiggling his fingers in Tchaka's face as the ball slides through the net, Hartstein turns to his two assistant coaches and exults, "Jesus, this kid's the real thing! Getting Stephon is like trading for an experienced senior point guard just when you need him! Do you realize Stephon could keep us in TV tournaments for the next four years?" There is in the coach's usually subdued voice something like joy.

"Stephon may be the real thing, but you'd better watch him right from the start," warns Gerard Bell, one of Hartstein's assistants. "Stephon's got that attitude. When he walked in today, he gave me the Marbury look. I'm telling you now; you better not start him the first game. I don't want another four years of Norman."

"Don't worry," Hartstein assures Bell. "Stephon's gonna

be okay. He's a lot more down to earth than his brothers. He's seen three of them struggle. He's not gonna make the same mistakes."

"Yeah, well, Donnie saw one brother struggle, Norman saw two, and it didn't help them," Bell replies.

•

After practice all the players tumble down the school's front steps into the cool October air. Tchaka heads south a few blocks toward the subway for the long ride back to Queens. Stephon walks up to me and says, "Take me to Micky D's. I'm hungry. I could eat three Big Macs. You got any cash?" I've already agreed to drive Russell and Corey home, so I tell Stephon that I'll take him as well. But the idea of being driven around Coney Island in my creaky, two-door Toyota apparently isn't what Stephon had in mind. "This is your ride?" he says in disbelief as he walks up to my car. "Man, you got to get yourself some new wheels. When I get to college, I'm gonna get me a white Nissan Sentra — that shit is *milk!*"

"Just get in the damn car," Russell says.

Stephon makes a move toward the front seat, but Russell swiftly intercepts him. "Six-foot-three gets the front," he commands. "Five-foot-nine goes in back." Corey wisely stays out of it. He puts his Walkman on, pops the hatch, and climbs in the far back, smiling to himself as if enjoying some private joke.

Russell is in no mood right now for Stephon's mouth. In the past few weeks, as Rick Barnes and the other college coaches kept flocking to see Tchaka, new recruiting interest in Russell began to dry up. Not only that, but several schools that had been pursuing Russell in September suddenly backed off. No sooner did Russell make up his mind to sign with Cal-Irvine than its coach, Rod Baker, called Hartstein at school to say he was no longer interested

— the guard he thought was leaving had decided to come back. That was that. Then Bob Wenzel, the head coach at Rutgers, who had been expressing his interest in Russell ever since the Empires, dropped by Lincoln — but announced that he would meet only with Tchaka. Finally a Duquesne coach worked Russell into a state of agitated excitement by promising to watch him play at the Garden, but when the big day arrived the coach stood him up. It was hard to know for sure what was going on, but evidently some coaches were convinced that Russell had too far to go to reach 700 on his SATs (coaches somehow learned of his test scores before he'd even had time to show them to his mother), and others kept changing their minds about what sort of player to recruit. This, of course, was precisely what Russell had feared all along. And with each school that courted and then abandoned him he seemed to go through the full cycle of infatuation, falling in love, rejection, and painful recuperation; each time he survived with a little less of the spirit to forge on with the school year. "I don't know what's going on," Russell said to me before today's practice. "They were recruiting me, but now they're not. I haven't heard from any of them in weeks."

•

Autumn is arriving quickly this year in Coney Island. For weeks the clouds have come across the water low and gray, and the trees along Ocean Parkway are already bare. As I drive toward McDonald's with the players in my car, we splash through piles of trash and fallen leaves. "If you crash and I get injured, Coach is gonna kill you," Stephon advises me from the back seat. "That'll be four years down the drain." Then he announces, to no one in particular, "When I go to college, I'm going to Syracuse or Georgia Tech."

"How come?" I ask.

"Because at Syracuse you play in front of thirty-two-thousand, eight-hundred-and-twenty people every home game — it's crazy-loud in there," he says, meaning the Syracuse Carrier Dome. "And because Georgia Tech knows how to treat its point guards." Stephon is no doubt thinking of Kenny Anderson — the player he is most often compared with — who left Georgia Tech after his sophomore year and just signed a five-season, $14.5 million contract with the New Jersey Nets. Anderson's salary is a figure Stephon knows as precisely as he does the seating capacity of the Carrier Dome.

Driving along, we pass beneath the elevated train tracks over Stillwell Avenue. There is a lot of commercial activity on this block, catering mostly to the summer crowds who take the subway here on their way to the beach and the amusement park. But once we get past Stillwell, the shops and pedestrians grow scarcer block by block. The train tracks are considered the official start of the Coney Island peninsula; beyond them are the projects, and few store owners will risk doing business out there. The McDonald's near Stillwell is pretty much the last outpost of franchise food before the streets lose their commercial appeal and plunge into the shadow of the high-rises.

Elbowing his way to the counter, Stephon orders two Big Macs, two large fries, a chocolate shake, an ice cream sundae, and waits for me to pick up the tab. Russell accepts my offer of a burger and fries. Corey, as always, pays his own way. With our food in hand, we pile back into my car.

Stephon, hungrily consuming his first burger, wedges himself between the two front seats in order to speak directly into Russell's ear. "So," he says, "what are they offering you?"

Russell angrily snatches his head away and stares out the

window; from this spot along Mermaid Avenue, the projects and acres of rubble-strewn lots loom in front of us like an abandoned city, Dresden after the war.

"You mean you're just gonna sign?" Stephon goes on. "And then when you get to campus and see all them players driving those nice white Nissan Sentras, what you gonna say to yourself? 'Oh well, I guess they got them from their *mothers'*?" Stephon takes another bite of his burger. "That's just like Tchaka. All these coaches coming around, and he ain't asking for *anything*. Not even a guaranteed starting position. That's *crazy!* He gonna get to campus and everybody on the team gonna be driving cars except him! He's gonna be, like, 'Excuse me but five guys got cars here!'"

Russell shifts uneasily in the seat beside me. He professes not to care, but in fact Russell hates to hear the stories that have been circulating lately about kids offered inducements to sign with certain colleges or players at other high schools who never study and get "passed along" in their classes; it offends his belief in the meritocracy of basketball. "By the way, Stephon," he says, "the NCAA does *not* allow players to get cars."

"Ha! You think the NCAA gives a fuck about cars?" Stephon, still with his head next to Russell's, gives a high, piercing laugh. "Why do you think the best players go where they go? 'Cause the schools promise to take care of them and their families. They say the magic word — *money.*" Not getting the reaction he desires from Russell, Stephon turns his attention to me. "I'd rather hear 'no' than not ask and have some other guy come along and get some. You know what I mean? If you don't ask, you don't get. Like if I wasn't getting my burn" — his playing time — "here at Lincoln? I'd be, like, later for this. I'd be up and out with quickness."

Russell has finally had enough. He palms Stephon's little head with his giant hand and dunks him into the back seat.

"Stephon, why don't you start acting like a freshman, which is what you are."

"I ain't heard Coach say that yet," comes Stephon's swift reply.

•

It's no secret around Lincoln where Stephon gets his head for business. Last summer, when I was at the B/C camp in Gettysburg, I ran into Stephon's father, Donald Marbury. "You the guy writing about Lincoln?" he asked me one day. "And you haven't even interviewed Mr. Lincoln Basketball himself?" He shook my hand warmly, and when I told him how much I wanted to speak with him, a sly smile played across his creased and handsome face. "Well, in that case I expect there will be some gratuities for me and my family." I must have looked surprised, because the smile disappeared and Mr. Marbury snapped angrily, "Oh, come on now! Bobby Hartstein didn't have a winning season until the Marburys started going there. If it weren't for me and my boys, Lincoln wouldn't have any notoriety. It wouldn't even be worth writing about!"

I had been warned that dealing with Mr. Marbury might have its complications. Years ago, when he first began showing up at Lincoln to watch his son Eric play, he would stand at the sidelines yelling at Hartstein, "Put my son in! That's why you're losing!" So the school's athletic director started assigning a teacher to sit next to Mr. Marbury in the bleachers in order to prevent him from cursing at the ref; he was sometimes one obscenity shy of drawing a technical foul. Whatever predisposition Mr. Marbury showed for angry outbursts, however, has only grown over the years, as Eric, then Donnie, and finally Norman tried to make it — if not to the NBA, then at least through graduation day at a four-year school — only to fall short of those aspirations. Now Mr. Marbury was down to his last basketball-playing son, and whether it came from his belief in Stephon's marketability or his fear of being haunted by yet another set of abandoned dreams, Mr. Marbury seemed ready to cash in now. "Unfortunately, my first three boys didn't reach the ultimate plateau, but I got another chance with Stephon," he said to me in Pennsylvania. "He might be the first Lincoln player to go high Division One, you know. And if you want information about that, I expect that you will have the money to pay for it."

Warned or not, I didn't actually expect Mr. Marbury to ask me for hard cash, and all I could think to say at the time was that most journalists considered it unethical to pay people for information; deals like that would cast doubt on the credibility of their reporting. Mr. Marbury shrugged dismissively. "I'm not like all them other Coney Island guys — too stupid to know the value of what they're sitting on." He tapped his brow. "This is a business — ain't nothing but. And if I don't receive satisfaction, I will take my business somewhere else. I always say, a wise man has his wisdom to protect him. A fool has his God." A hostile silence fell between us, and we quickly parted company.

Toward the end of the summer, I ran into Mr. Marbury again. Once more I asked to interview him, and again he stated his terms: I was free to write about Stephon, but if I wanted the Marburys' exclusive story, I was going to have to make him an offer. "You think Patrick Ewing or Michael Jordan gave away their stories for nothing?" he scoffed. "Maybe I should get a ghostwriter and tell my *own* story. That's my share of the glory, you know." Again I raised my concern about paying people for their cooperation. This time Mr. Marbury started laughing at me. "Is that right!" he said, smirking and folding his arms across his chest. "I guess that's why I saw you buying all that stuff for Corey and Russell." I didn't have the slightest idea what he was talking about. "Yeah, that's right," he said, his eyes enlarging. "At the Seven-Eleven in Gettysburg: I saw you buying them slushies!" He leaned toward me, his voice bitterly sarcastic. "And now I suppose you want me to think you did it because you're just a nice guy. *Oh, come on!*"

So that was it: Mr. Marbury had confused me with a college coach and the occasional snacks I bought the players with those under-the-table deals he had read so much about.

The coaches who recruited the Marbury boys over the years have said that Donald Marbury "just won't stop dining out on his sons' talent," that he "thinks he knows the game better than he does," and if he keeps it up he will "get himself into trouble with the NCAA." As for Stephon, the coaches are starting to complain that he's just like his father — a player looking to "get over," to take advantage of any situation. In certain circles, the Marburys are considered the avatars of all that is most unseemly about high school basketball. "They've been taught that you rape 'em, you get whatever you can," lamented one summer-league coach (who tried, unsuccessfully, to recruit Stephon for his own team). "Everybody wants a deal. No one plays for the love of the game anymore." At the time Mr. Marbury and I had our confrontation about the slushies, I couldn't have agreed more.

But now, having spent several months with Stephon, I am beginning to wonder how he and his father are supposed to act. The entire basketball establishment has been trying to buy Stephon for years: summer-league teams like the Gauchos pay his way to tournaments around the country (last summer found him as far away as Arizona); street agents take Stephon into the Knicks' and Nets' locker rooms for chats with the pros; basketball camps give him a bountiful supply of T-shirts, trophies, sneakers, bags, and caps; and coaches on every level constantly lay on hands, hoping to win his affection. (This, of course, is just a reprise of how the coaches treated Stephon's brothers — until they encountered academic difficulties, at which point the coaches abruptly withdrew their affection and largess.) And lately, in the coaches' efforts to appropriate Stephon, they have been trying to buy his father. Last year a summer coach for whom Stephon occasionally played found Mr. Marbury some part-time work; and the reason I ran into him at the B/C camp last summer is that administrators, hoping to enroll Stephon, had given his father a summer coaching job. So when Stephon tells Russell that coaches "take care of the players and their families," he knows whereof he speaks.

Mr. Marbury thinks that Stephon and I are playing the same game, and in the paradigm in which we are operating, I suppose we are. When I first met Stephon, he asked me for seventy-five cents for the school's juice machine. When he found out I planned to write a book about the Lincoln team, he announced: "Every day I'm hitting you up. I'm just warning you." Hartstein shuddered whenever he overheard his young star making such demands and muttered to himself about how difficult it was to deal with the Marbury clan, but Stephon operated as his father did — without apology. He would stand in front of me, blocking my path, waiting for me to fork it over. And I would. At the time it didn't seem like much — seventy-five cents; big deal. But now, having watched the recruiters at work — "Twenty dollars' Christmas money," Jim Boeheim would say. "Big deal" — I'm beginning to feel a little like a college coach myself. (Maybe that's why getting pulled into Rick Barnes's recruiting pitch left such a bad taste in my mouth; one hates to be caught out in public that way.) At any rate, Mr. Marbury is holding out for a deal. I can see why he thinks I'm getting over on him. And now, as I drive down Mermaid Avenue with the players in my car and watch in my rearview mirror as Stephon puts away the second Big Mac I just bought him, I wonder whether there isn't some way I can meet his father's demands after all.

•

By the time I reach the tag end of the Coney Island peninsula, where Corey, Russell, and Stephon live, everyone has finished his burgers and fries and we ride down the last stretch of Mermaid in silence. Given its current state of bombed-out desolation, it is hard to imagine that twenty years ago this street was full of businesses, just as the residential areas in Coney Island once had stand-alone houses and hopeful homeowners. During the urban-renewal years, however, the city knocked down not only all the houses in this neighborhood but also most of the storefronts along Mermaid. The strategy was to punch one hole in each block and wait for the rest to self-destruct; then the city could take over all the buildings for nonpayment of taxes. The blocks did fall apart, but once the city moved tenants into the projects, it abandoned much of its commercial-redevelopment plan. Now the only signs of life on some blocks are the drunks leaning against the plywood of boarded-up buildings and the mangy dogs scavenging vacant lots. It's a sorry enough sight that some buildings on adjacent streets were deliberately built without windows facing Mermaid so that residents could more easily avert their gaze.

It's not yet six P.M. by the time I reach Russell's building, but some of Coney Island's drug dealers have already taken to the streets. A lot of the dealers in this part of the neighborhood spend their days hanging out by the fried chicken store on Mermaid Avenue, drinking in curbside posses and discussing which new homie will rise to the top while the old guard serves its time in prison. Then they get to work around this time, fanning out into the neighborhood like a night brigade, pausing in front of double-parked cars, disappearing down streets and alleyways when the occasional cop car comes along.

Russell spots a kid he used to play with at the Garden loping down a project walkway with a rangy gait and his Georgetown cap on backward. "Look at him," he says sadly. "Just doing the same ol' same ol'. Shoot 'em up. Bang-bang."

Simply put, in Coney Island there is basketball, and when that doesn't work out, there are drugs. And despite all the efforts of Disco and Mr. Lou to separate the two, the wall seems to have been breached, with washed-up players like Chocolate joining the gangs and getting killed, and dealers disrupting games among the serious players in order to show off their playground moves. "That's all they do," Russell says, watching his erstwhile friend disappear down the alley. "And if they ain't talking or shooting each other, they're trying to bring the players down." He turns to me and says his next words slowly and deliberately so that I won't fail to grasp their import. "This is the toughest area to come up in. It really is. 'Cause once you veer off like them, you're stuck. Maybe you have another chance, but it's a little less than you had before. 'Cause what's here today can easily fall away." With that, Russell climbs out of my car with his omnipresent stack of SAT review books under his arm. "Those guys ain't doing nothing with their lives, so they don't want you to be doing nothing either," he says through the open car window. "But when we're in college, they'll still be in the parks, saying the same thing to someone else. Man, I hate Coney Island. Ain't nothing gonna change around here except maybe the faces. After I get to college, I am *never* coming back. Until then, boys" — he gives us a weary salute — "I'm staying inside."

I drive down the block to drop off Stephon and Corey.

They live on the fourth and fifth floors of the same building, directly over the Garden. Corey climbs out of the car and takes off, whistling the theme song of "Jeopardy." Then Stephon gets out. After leaning into the window to slap my hand, he starts walking toward his building with that King Marbury stride. I watch as he swaggers across the deserted playground, trailing his hand along the jungle gym. A bunch of guys in their twenties, drinking their afternoon beers, call out to him as he goes by.

On the streets and courts of Coney Island, Stephon is a legend in his own time. In fact, it may not be too much to say that he is the most gifted freshman point guard right now in the entire country. But for at least another five years, the benefits of his extraordinary talent will accrue only to those people who gather around him, angling for a piece of the action — high school and college coaches, camp directors and sneaker company executives. And though practically every stitch of clothing Stephon owns has been given to him by a coach as a down payment on future services, there remain dozens of obstacles between him and his dream of playing in front of 32,820 fans at the Syracuse Carrier Dome.

Meanwhile, Stephon returns each night to this neighborhood where the only people who own white Nissan Sentras are the drug dealers, and to this building, an X-shaped slab of concrete rising fourteen stories into the air. I've spent some time in Stephon's building, and it's not the most pleasant place to come home to after a long practice, whether or not a coach or a reporter has just bought you a meal at Micky D's. The elevator seldom works; the long halls reek of urine; the dark stairwells, where the dealers lurk, echo with the low rumble of drug transactions. The steel apartment doors don't even have numbers on them, adding to the sense of menace and confusion, though they must have at one time because just outside the Marburys' apartment someone has scrawled across the wall I WANNA FUCK THE GIRL IN 3B CAUSE SHE SUCKS DICK GOOD. I've never been inside the Marburys' apartment, but according to a rumor circulating among the coaches at the B/C camp last summer, the family owns so little furniture that recruiters in pursuit of Norman a few years ago had to give their pitch standing up. Dealing with squalor like that, of course, is what makes recruiting such an arduous business.

Eight

EVERY LINCOLN PLAYER has his own beguiling vision of what the college experience will be like. For Stephon it involves crazy-loud crowds, star treatment at point, and, as with Kenny Anderson, an early bid at the pro draft. Russell wishes ardently for a "nice small tight school where they'll look after me and I can get my degree in nursing and I'll never have to come back to Coney Island." Corey, though his image requires that he rarely talk about it, once let slip, "I've been thinking of going to a Southern school — Florida State, North Carolina, maybe Virginia. I hate it when it gets sharp and brisk out like it does here. My one rule is, I won't go anyplace where I got to wear one of them Eskimo coats." And Tchaka wants, more than anything, to find a school where he can develop his offensive skills, secure a starting spot, climb up the NCAA rankings, and maybe have a shot at the pros himself.

Tchaka must have had a premonition that the promised land was near at hand, because the night before he was scheduled to visit the Seton Hall campus, as we made plans on the phone to drive there in my car, he sounded unusually nervous — as jittery, in fact, as he had before his trip to the Nike camp.

"What are you going to be looking for?" I asked.

"Oh, you know — see the life, what to expect if I go there."

"Do you know what you're going to wear?"

"I thought I should get a little dressed up to impress them," he replied thoughtfully. "Maybe wear some sneaks." There was silence on the line. "Do you think I can bring Steve along? He's my buddy, you know."

The next morning, when I go to pick him up, Tchaka has given up on the idea of inviting Steve, but he is looking sharp in black nylon sweatpants, a Nike T-shirt, and black Air Jordans. He tells me he's been up since four, doing his laundry. He downs a quick glass of strawberry milk for good luck, and the two of us drive from Queens to Seton Hall University, just outside Newark, New Jersey.

Seton Hall is one of those small schools which seem to have been built around their athletic facilities. This is rather fitting, since few had ever heard of Seton Hall until P. J. Carlesimo became head coach in 1982 and built its perennially losing basketball program into one of the finest in the Big East. Today, Carlesimo has arranged for Tchaka to be given a tour of the entire campus — the classrooms, dorms, and libraries — but as it turns out, most of our time is clocked precisely where Tchaka will spend it if he does attend Seton Hall next year: the Brennan Recreation Center.

Our guide for the day will be the assistant coach Tom Sullivan. Tall, lanky, with a modified Ted Koppel haircut, Sullivan covets Tchaka's signature on a Seton Hall letter-of-intent form with an ardor equal to his competitors', but thus far he has kept a respectful distance. Sullivan is a former Fordham basketball star, and however much he may swoon over Tchaka's play on the court, when he is with the recruit he affects a laconic, lawyerly manner that contrasts immediately with the more baroque styles of Massimino and Barnes; he keeps his eagerness in check.

"Let me show you our arena," he says to Tchaka, "though I'm sure you've seen it plenty of times on TV." From Coach Carlesimo's office, Sullivan leads us down several long, narrow corridors in the bowels of the recreation center to a short, low-ceilinged gangway, and there — all of a sudden — it is: the Seton Hall Pirates' gym. At this early hour, the place is as empty and still as a Sunday morning — no crowds, no ref's whistle, not even a ball bouncing off the rim — and Sullivan reserves comment while Tchaka walks tentatively onto the hardwood and examines the polished parquet floor, the Big East banners hanging above one basket, and the thousands upon thousands of bright, empty seats rising steeply to the rafters. It feels as if we've boarded the deck of an aircraft carrier in drydock.

After a couple of minutes of this, Sullivan says, "Let's take a look at the rest of the place, shall we?" Back we go down the labyrinthine corridors until we reach the Seton Hall players' locker room. Or is it a men's club? The royal blue carpeting (Pirates' colors) is lawn-thick, and the oak-grained lockers gleam under deep custodial care like wainscotting in the Edwardian Room. Above each locker hangs a colored portrait of a player on the team, superimposed over a picture of a basketball. In the middle of the room, two gray leather couches are arranged before a state-of-the-art TV and video system. By and large it marks an improvement over the drafty basement digs where the Lincoln players change for their games.

"You're six-seven; is that right?" Sullivan asks. Tchaka nods. "Well, you'll find these lockers are built for you." Like a well-schooled maître d', the coach opens a locker and points to its array of shelves, most of them at Tchaka's eye level. "The guards come in and say, 'How'm I supposed to get up here?' Don't matter." Sullivan swats the air. "We don't want guards. We want guys like you." Tchaka slowly circles the room, running his hand over the smooth wood, the supple leather. Sullivan stands with his arms crossed, letting Tchaka roam as he pleases.

Our next stop on tour is the players' weight room. "We

insist our guys work out," Sullivan explains. "Nothin' fancy. Just give me plates and bars and let me see how much you can put in the air." Even at midmorning, several Pirates are groaning at their exertions, and Sullivan nods casually toward the sweating bodies. "In our league, Tchaka, you can never factor out strength. The Big East is a rarefied level. Every day you're going up against the best." Sullivan lowers his voice confidentially. "And from this league, Tchaka, you can go on to the next one." This must come as music to Tchaka's ears. Sullivan is the first coach to say out loud that he thinks Tchaka could play in the pros.

Our host is now leading us back through the maze of corridors to a small office equipped with three VCRs, a TV, and a computer. As we take seats around a long conference table, Sullivan pops in a promotional tape, "Seton Hall Basketball: A Great Experience On and Off the Court." Aerial shots of the leafy, suburban campus dissolve, one over another, as various student-athletes provide testimonials: "I love the campus life . . . I chose Seton Hall because of the family-type atmosphere . . . Our academic adviser, I call her my mother away from home . . ." Then the deep-voiced narrator returns to explain that "the Pirates play their home games at one of the East Coast's premier facilities — the Brendan Byrne Arena at the Meadowlands," which, we are told, once held "the largest crowd ever to see a college basketball game." Sullivan hits the pause button. "Yeah, we own that number," he says.

Next, Sullivan guides Tchaka's attention toward the computer analyzer. With this, the coach explains, the team's technical wizards will take tapes of, say, a Georgetown game and string together ten examples of the Hoyas inbounding the ball. Then the Seton Hall team will study all ten plays in a row to familiarize themselves with their opposition. Sullivan turns back to the recruit. "At this level, Tchaka, basketball takes on a complexity. Some are ready, some are not. We try to give you as much information as you need to win. Not because we're just nice guys" — Sullivan looks Tchaka in the eye, and Tchaka is all there, listening to every word — "but because we like to win too.

"I saw you play in that Boys Club tournament in Virginia," he continues, seguing nicely from one winning moment to another. "I saw you hitting those fade-away baseline jumpers." For a moment, Tchaka looks puzzled — he's not sure he ever hit a fade-away baseline jumper in his life — but who wouldn't enjoy the image that comes to mind? "Oh, yeah, that's right." Sullivan nods. "Now of course at Seton Hall you'll be playing a power game —" A flicker of concern passes over Tchaka's face. Sullivan notes this and makes a quick clarification: "But our power forwards shoot the ball just as much as our smaller guys do." Tchaka smiles, which makes Sullivan smile. "And I know you're up to it. I've seen not just your moments of brilliance, but your games of brilliance too."

At the end of the tour, P. J. Carlesimo himself — red-bearded, ever-intense, and wearing his trademark Nike sweater vest — emerges from his inner sanctum to greet Tchaka. While Tchaka stands with his hands clasped in front of him and a beatific expression on his face, Carlesimo and Sullivan have a brief, studied exchange about one of their former players who was recently drafted into the pros.

CARLESIMO: Where's he going?

SULLIVAN: Portland.

CARLESIMO: Oh, yeah. Signed a big contract with them, didn't he?

SULLIVAN: *Very* big.

After the tour is over, Tchaka tells me he has worked up a killer appetite, so we head over to a pizza joint just off campus. When we walk in, we see a young couple engaged in some amorous business in a corner booth and a pretty girl about Tchaka's age standing behind the counter. As soon as

Tchaka goes over to place his order, she asks whether he's a Seton Hall player. "Might be," Tchaka says coyly.

"Well, I hope you'll decide to come," she says. "If you do, I'll be seeing you around." The girl smiles demurely, then disappears to fetch our pizza. (Am I indulging in conspiracy theories, or does the recruiting never end?)

I glance up at Tchaka. He looks down at me. For a moment he seems unable to speak, rendered mute with excitement. Then a huge smile spreads across his face, and he lifts his arms in an embrace that seems to take in the whole place — the campus, the gym, the plush locker room, perhaps even this good-will ambassador behind the counter, now returning with our food. "It's *fly*, D!" he cries. "It's *crazy*-fly!"

As I carry our loaded tray across the restaurant, Tchaka rubs his palms together, the future now his to reach out and grasp. "Seton Hall is *the* up-and-coming team in the Big East," he says. "I'll pay my dues as a freshman, start when I'm a sophomore, and be a team leader by my junior year. *Then*" — he claps his hands together, and the couple in the corner shoots him a caustic look — "maybe win a national championship when I'm a senior."

We settle into a booth and Tchaka begins enumerating all the reasons he should sign with Seton Hall and, at the same time, maniacally shaking hot peppers on his pizza. "I like it here. They were straight up with me. Told me exactly where I would fit in — no funny business."

He rains more peppers down on his slice.

"I won't have to spend all my time posting up against the big guys. They'll let me face the basket. And by junior year they'll probably move me to small forward."

I try to alert Tchaka to the volume of peppers he is deploying, but I can't get his attention.

"It just doesn't feel right when you say the name Providence or Villanova. But Seton Hall? Now that brings a smile to my face."

Not to mention even more peppers on his pizza.

"Where you goin' to college?" he asks himself. "Goin' to Seton Hall," he replies. "*Word!*"

His pizza is now officially inedible.

"I can see the headline when I sign: PIRATES GET THEIR SHIPP." Tchaka laughs, hoists his mountainous slice with two hands, opens wide, and (Don't do it!) inserts. A pound of gravelly peppers glides down his throat. Not even pizza flambé could get his attention now.

•

Heading toward Thanksgiving, Lincoln High could not have asked for greater success from its varsity basketball team. Even as school administrators are struggling to control a rash of violent encounters in the hallways and a new trend that has seen several Lincoln kids jumped by rival gangs right outside the school building, Tchaka, Russell, Corey, and Stephon are bringing acclaim to their beleaguered school. They are undefeated in all their games and scrimmages so far. They are making headlines in the sports pages of all the New York tabloids with their blistering, fast-break offense. They even earn an invitation to fly to San Diego for the Above the Rim Christmas tournament of the country's top sixteen high school teams. Lincoln isn't just winning either; as the team travels by subway to its away games around the city, Tchaka, Russell, Corey, and Stephon are blowing out their opponents by such lopsided scores that opposing coaches often shake their heads after the final buzzer and remark, "Those guys were *high school* players?"

Russell seems to be scoring at will; in the team's first scrimmage he turned in an outrageous 46-point performance, missing only three of twenty-four field-goal attempts, then kept up a 25-point pace for the next several games. *The Hoop Scoop* ranked him the sixth best player in all of New York City, he earned an honorable mention in *Street & Smith's* nationwide basketball roundup, and an influential scouting report dubbed him the "Secretary of Defense" for his smothering play at the opposite end of the court.

As for Stephon, he is getting his burn, and then some. To no one's surprise, Hartstein started him in the season's first game (fifteen points, twelve assists) and every one thereafter. *Newsday,* under a half-page picture of the Lincoln team holding the smiling young point guard in their arms, announced that "the era of Stephon Marbury" had begun. "The fourth Marbury brother to play at Lincoln — and, possibly, the most talented — Stephon has transformed supreme confidence into out-and-out giddiness," the article reported. "Asked what he will bring to Lincoln this year, Marbury responded, 'Another Kenny Anderson.'" Actually Stephon is ahead of his idol's pace; not even Anderson started as a high school freshman. College scouting reports are already giving Stephon their highest rating. An assistant coach from Providence came down to watch Stephon practice one day, waving discreetly to the freshman — and thereby violating the intent, if not the letter, of NCAA rules designed to protect underclassmen from recruiters. ("It's never too early to start showing interest," the coach whispered.) Word of Stephon's prowess even reached a TV production company, which contacted him about making a commercial, though when the NCAA informed the Marburys that accepting a fee might violate its rules, his father declined. Everyone keeps checking to see if the legendary Marbury bravado will affect Stephon's game — before the season, even some of his teammates were hoping that an opposing point guard would bust him just once, to lower his ego. But Stephon has not only established himself as a superb floor general, able to marshal all the talent on this team into one brutally effective offensive force; he has become, while the seniors are distracted by their recruiting, the team's de facto leader. Stephon is working harder than anyone in practice and has no qualms about dressing down his older friends if they don't match his effort.

But off the court, it is impossible not to notice how dramatically Tchaka's fortunes seem to be diverging from those of his Coney Island teammates.

Corey is still writing verse, and writing it well. The other day he showed me a poem about life in Coney Island that ended, "A place meant for happiness, sweet love and care — / Something any human desires to share. / Yet it seems to haunt instead of praise / The foundation and center of our bitter days." Corey is amazingly prolific, often dashing off a new poem for every girl he meets. But having merged his twin passions — writing and romance — he rarely leaves time for his homework. He does the assignments he likes, ignores the rest, and, though he never causes trouble in class or makes excuses for his bad grades — especially during first-period classes, which is a telltale sign that he's not struggling with the work, just sleeping late — his average remains just above 65. Three times Corey told Coach Hartstein he was taking the SATs, and never did. "That's just his style," Russell explained the other day. "He don't care about nothing till the last minute; then he be flippin'." But already several Division I coaches have identified Corey as a gifted player whose grades, if he doesn't pull them out of the fire right away, will be his undoing.

Meanwhile Stephon, despite his supreme self-confidence on the court, often seems oppressed by the pressure put on him not only to succeed in his own right, but to redeem his entire family. Disappointment over the careers of Eric, Donnie, and Norman has never dissipated in Coney Island; sometimes when I stand around the Lincoln corridors, I hear talk about nothing but how "Spoon, Sky, and Jou-Jou should have all gone big time. Why didn't it work out for any of them?" Even the school custodian stops Stephon in the hallway after practice one day to advise him, "Work hard, okay? Don't fuck up like your brothers."

The day that happens, Stephon asks me for a lift into downtown Brooklyn so that he can catch the subway to Manhattan for a Knicks game. Heading northward on Ocean Parkway, we climb steadily up Brooklyn's socioeconomic ladder, from the Coney Island projects at one end through several bustling Hassidic neighborhoods and on into Park Slope, a middle-class neighborhood of tree-lined streets and well-kept brownstones. Watching the affluent world slide by our window, Stephon grows quiet for a while, playing absently with his earring. When he speaks again, it is in a quiet, contemplative voice I have never heard from him before. "You know, when I was a little kid, I wanted to do everything exactly like my older brothers, even the stupid things. I wanted to be just like them — Norman especially." Stephon gives a small, hard laugh, as if looking back over the span of many years. "But that isn't true anymore. I want to take a different route than he did. I'm gonna pass my SATs and go to a four-year school and make it all the way. Everybody's always saying I'm just like Jou-Jou, but that's not fair. I'm *not* like Jou-Jou. I'm nothing like him. Not about this, anyway." Stephon shakes his head — angry at the comparison and saddened that it has become something to disavow. "I still think Norman could get recruited to a Division One school and then maybe go pro in the hardship draft. Well, I don't know. But it's true what people say: Norman didn't do anything his freshman year at Lincoln. He just went to class and went to sleep. He woke up in his sophomore year, but his freshman year really hurt him. I'm working hard *right now*." Stephon seems to know already that part of what success will require of him is the strength to separate from his family, forge a different path in life — a painful prospect at any age, but especially so at fourteen, when he should be worrying about nothing more consequential than whether he will grow tall enough in the next year or two to dunk.

Stephon *is* showing incredible determination in his classes, just as he does on the court. He spends hours on the phone at night with his math tutor, and he even turned down Coach Hartstein's recent offer to transfer him to an easier math class, where his grade would no doubt improve. Unfortunately, hard work alone — although it is preached endlessly to the players as the one sure route to success — does not suffice in these circumstances. Despite Stephon's efforts, his English teachers notice that his book reports rarely include a complete sentence or period or capital letter — not a good omen for the verbal portion of the SATs. And his math teacher spots huge gaps in his basic understanding that must be caught now, before they get any worse.

The same thing is happening with Russell. He still studies each and every night for the SATs, and he scores reasonably well on practice exams. Coach Hartstein even got him a private tutor and a scholarship to a Stanley Kaplan class. But there is so much riding on this test — all Russell's dreams of making it to a four-year school — and he has acquired such poor fundamental skills over the years, that when test day arrives, Russell's concentration vanishes. He does something he never does on the court: he panics. And then he forgets all he has recently learned, which shakes his enduring faith that hard work can indeed win the day. "I *know* I can pass that test. I just get *so* nervous," he said the other day. "I took it again last weekend. I *think* I came through. But I don't know. At this point, I just don't give a fuck."

When Tchaka scored 700 on his second SAT attempt last

June, I assumed at the time that his teammates would soon follow. Since then, however, I have learned how unusual is Tchaka's academic success — not only among his current teammates, but among all those Lincoln players over the years who aspired to four-year colleges. Tchaka, in fact, has set a number of unusual records at Lincoln. He is the first player ever to meet his college-eligibility requirements in his junior year of high school. He is the first player in sound enough academic shape to get his recruiting mail from Coach Hartstein before the end of his junior year. He is the first Lincoln player ever to attract, at one time or another, the interest of all the schools in the Big East conference. And he will soon become the first player in the school's long history to sign with a college in the fall of his senior year; most have waited until the following spring, hoping their grades and test scores would improve, and, when they didn't, have signed on with a junior college.

Sports psychologists and guidance counselors who work with inner-city athletes often talk about an essential triangle in a player's life formed by his family, his neighborhood, and his schooling. The rule is that a player can triumph over one weak point in that triangle, maybe two, but almost never all three. Tchaka has at least the first two in his favor — stability at home and in his neighborhood. Russell, Corey, and Stephon, however, all come from families that can't seem to escape their tenancy in the Coney Island projects. The neighborhood itself — with its armies of drug dealers and unwed teenage mothers — may be the least stable place in New York City in which to grow up. And now, as they face the hurdle of the SATs, it seems that years of bad schooling are coming back to haunt these athletes just when they need their educations the most. This may handicap them throughout their lives; on the immediate level, it means that while Tchaka is being taken on personal tours of the arenas and locker rooms of the Big East, Russell and

Corey have yet to go on a single campus recruiting visit, and their prospects of doing so look increasingly grim.

•

The NCAA and the college basketball industry have done much soul searching in recent years over the SAT requirement, as well they should. The NCAA instituted the 700 threshold, known as Proposition 48, in 1986, after coming under pressure to show its commitment to education as well as to athletics. But the requirement has proved to be an insurmountable obstacle to thousands of black players like Russell, Corey, and Stephon with poor educations and no experience in taking standardized tests. Of the players who have gone to junior colleges since the rule was instituted (they are known as Prop 48 casualties), 9 percent are white, 91 percent black. Some critics have suggested that if the NCAA is so concerned about the education of its student-athletes, it should allow a college to award scholarships to players who don't pass the SATs, as long as they stay off the team until the school brings them up to speed in the classroom. Or the NCAA might eliminate freshman eligibility across the board so that every player's first year in college would be devoted entirely to schoolwork. Or it could deny a school its coveted Division I status if its players didn't graduate. Then, the argument goes, instead of punishing educationally disadvantaged kids like the Coney Island players, the rules would punish the colleges with a weak commitment to academics. At the very least the NCAA could examine indications of a player's scholastic potential besides standardized tests — high school transcripts, say, or attendance records. But so far the NCAA has yet to embrace any options that might compel colleges to educate their players, only ones that flaunt the organization's lofty commitment to academics while they actually prevent many hard-working but poorly schooled athletes from getting a college education. Russell's school average of over 80, his practice of sitting in the first row of class and asking provocative questions, the estimation of his remedial math teacher that he works harder than any student she has had in thirty years — all of these things speak volumes about Russell's determination to succeed on the college level, but unless he gets a 700, they alone will get him nowhere.

The NCAA's rulebook governing the recruiting process goes on for forty-four pages and includes, in addition to Proposition 48, such arcana as the prohibition of recruiting tapes and multicolored brochures. The college coaches often say that if you don't break any rules, it's probably by accident; or, alternatively, if you use common sense, you're sure to get yourself into trouble. Of course, the coaches have their own reasons for condemning the NCAA rules — principally, that recruiting would be a lot easier if there *were* no rules — but on grounds of sheer capriciousness, it's hard to disagree with them. After I tagged along on Tchaka's visit to Seton Hall, apparently the NCAA's Kansas City headquarters faxed a notice to several other Big East schools that were recruiting him, instructing their coaches to bar me from accompanying Tchaka on any further campus visits. The spokeswoman I reached in Kansas City explained that the NCAA's ruling was made to protect Tchaka's interests: my presence on campus could be construed as an unfair recruiting advantage for one of the schools. I couldn't quite follow that argument and wondered whether the ruling couldn't also be construed as an advantage for the NCAA, which would be spared the embarrassment of having its excessive recruiting rituals so closely observed by a reporter. The NCAA, after all, serves two functions at once: to police the recruiters and to minimize the bad publicity that recruiting violations inevitably bring to the college game.

That was not my only run-in with the NCAA. After my several conversations with Donald Marbury, I decided to draw up a contract stipulating that all the players' families would share in whatever profit this book might make. At that point, however, the NCAA informed me that any arrangement I might make with the Lincoln players would violate their status as amateur athletes and jeopardize their eligibility to play NCAA ball.

Those two decisions — the one preventing me from observing Tchaka's campus visits, the other prohibiting my financial arrangement with the players — seem to encapsulate perfectly the corrupt theology of the NCAA. Purportedly, the NCAA maintains its strict standards of amateurism because it believes that a college scholarship is compensation enough for a player and that college sports should be treated as one more extracurricular activity, like playing tuba in the marching band. But if having a big-time college basketball program is really as tangential to a school's fortunes as the marching band or the fencing team, one wonders why the NCAA allows its basketball coaches to recruit their so-called amateur athletes by inviting them to campus, treating them to the finest restaurants, taking them to the best parties, and ushering them to courtside seats at the local pro franchises — all those subtle inducements I would have witnessed had the NCAA not banned me from visiting the other Big East campuses with Tchaka. And, given how many perks the NCAA does permit, I can't help thinking that it found my arrangement with the Lincoln players objectionable only because contractual deals like the one Mr. Marbury was demanding would do away with subtle inducements altogether and reveal college athletics for what it really is: commerce, pure and simple. Once that happens, however — once the whole business is measured in dollars and cents — it may seem considerably less defensible that poor black kids like Stephon should, for the price of a college scholarship and a few giveaways on campus, generate millions in ticket sales and TV contracts for the universities that recruit them simply because the NCAA and its member schools have a huge financial incentive in maintaining antiquated notions of the amateur athlete. (Even the Olympics are now filled with highly paid professionals and product endorsers.) The real issue, of course, is much simpler. Should college athletes receive a regular stipend for services rendered on the court? But addressing that question would also mean acknowledging the enormous inequity between these richly endowed colleges and their mostly impoverished players. So, instead, the NCAA investigates Syracuse for allegedly handing out twenty-dollar Christmas bonuses and deliberates over the use or misuse of muticolored stationery during the recruiting process.

•

After Russell took the SATs last weekend for what must be the fourth time, Terry was planning to treat him to a celebratory dinner at a restaurant in her neighhorhood. So as the players and I walk down the school steps after practice on the following Monday, I ask Russell whether he had a good time on his date.

"I dissed her good!" he roars. "You should have seen it. Tell him, Corey." Corey, walking next to Russell, doesn't say anything, so Russell goes on. "She came up to me all nice and sweet, and I said, 'Get out of my sight, Terry! Don't bother me no more!'"

I am stunned by this development. The last I had heard, Russell and Terry were doing great; in fact, she had asked him to draw up a list of colleges he was considering so that she could think about joining him when she graduated next year. ("Now I *got* to stay alive," Russell had said, "so I can be with Terry.") And the last time I saw the two of them together, Terry was sitting on Russell's lap in study hall, affectionately feeding him a bagel bite by bite.

"What were you fighting about?" I ask him.

"I don't know. I guess I was just in a bad mood because of the SATs." Russell drapes his arm over my shoulder. "Never let a girl see you sweat. Didn't your mother ever tell you that?" Russell emits a peculiar mirthless cackle. I look at Corey. He shrugs and traces a circle around his temple with his index finger.

It's late November now, and the days are getting shorter. By the time practice is over, the sun has long since dropped into its slot behind the Verrazano-Narrows Bridge, out past the western end of the Coney Island peninsula, and the sky at twilight is covered with bleak, wintery clouds. Since it's much too cold to hang out on the Coney Island courts, and no one feels like going straight home after practice, Russell, Corey, and Stephon often go over to Willie Johnson's barbershop on Flatbush Avenue, and I usually give them a lift on my way home.

Most nights now, as we drive past the brightly lit bodegas and rice-and-beans joints and used-car lots along Flatbush Avenue, the signs of approaching winter are upon us: homeless men sleeping over heating grates, and fires raging out of metal drums, circled by shivering men trying to keep warm. Everywhere we go in Brooklyn, we also pass nomadic groups of black teenagers, usually dressed like the Lincoln players, in high-tops and hooded sweatshirts. Tonight Corey looks out the car window and says in a high, fragile voice, "Oh, no. I just hate it when the Negroes wear those hoods. Scary! Oh! So scary!" Russell and Stephon burst out laughing, and Corey lifts his own hood over his head. He knows that when he walks around like that, cops will stop him on the street and pedestrians will turn away from him in fear. "Only in America," he says.

After the laughter subsides, Corey grows serious and brings up the subject of his older brother Louis, a.k.a. Sweet Lou, who is a freshman this year at the University of Buffalo. Evidently Louis and the team's other black players have faced so much harassment in Buffalo that Louis is considering transferring to a New York City school. "It's racial up there," Corey says. "He goes into stores and they make him stand in front, saying, 'What you want?' They won't let him go in. Now what kind of shit is that?"

"Damn! And Louis is a *light*-skinned nigger, too," Russell says. "What do you think they would do to someone with *my* complexion?" He covers his dark face with his hands. "Man, even if I pass my SATs, where am I gonna go? I can't go to Weber State — Utah's got the KKK and all those Mormons. Boston is racist, I hear, so forget about BC. Wichita's in the boondocks. And in Texas every time you walk out at night they say, 'Hey, nigger boy, what you want?' And they can do that, too, 'cause the sheriff's always in with them." Russell looks up morosely. "Man, I do *not* want to go some place where I'm not wanted. No way."

Corey's mention of his brother's Buffalo experience makes me realize how long it's been since I heard Corey talk about his own college plans. So I ask him the question I seem to have been avoiding — whether the continuing absence of visits and letters from the coaches is starting to worry him. He smiles and says, "Nah, Coach Hartstein got a whole boxful of mail for me. He's just keeping it — especially all the Big East mail — so I'll work harder." Apparently Corey's occasional peeks into Hartstein's mailbox continue to convince him of his good situation, although recently he's been getting far more form letters than personal appeals.

"Still got to pass those SATs," Russell warns bleakly.

"I'm not scared," Corey replies. "I do well on tests. Especially the vocabulary part. Anyway, we're seniors. This should be our year to relax."

"Yeah, if Corey don't get his seven hundred," Stephon assures me from the back seat, "he goin' to the *moon!*" This is the sort of admiring comment Corey would do well not to hear; he is starting to believe that his reputation as the team's smartest and coolest player grows in inverse proportion to the work he does in the classroom and the grades he receives. "That test is *hard*," Stephon goes on. "I looked at it once and almost fainted. I read somewhere that David Robinson got a thirteen hundred. Is that possible? Man, if I got that, I'd be the happiest guy in the world."

"I heard there are players now who get other guys to take the test for them," Russell says. He looks at me. "How do they get away with that? Find someone who looks like them?"

This is not a good sign. One of Russell's friends at Grady, who had been scoring lower than he on practice tests, suddenly got his 700 and signed with a top program; and some Lincolnites have begun wondering whether the Grady players are using stand-ins to take the test.

•

Business is brisk tonight at Willie's barbershop when we arrive; either that or a lot of guys are using the place to stay off the street and keep warm. Willie and his partner are cutting with dispatch, and still a half-dozen guys are hanging out, passing around the basketball that Willie keeps on hand and watching sitcom reruns on the TV. As a rule, Willie refuses to charge Russell or any family member for haircuts. "Unfortunately, that includes about half of Coney Island," he explains as we walk in the shop. Five of this year's twelve varsity players are cousins of the Johnson family; one project building in Coney Island has fourteen Johnson relatives spread among eleven floors. "They leave," Willie says with a sigh, "but more just come and take their place." What he loses in barbershop fees, though, he makes up for in family atmosphere. As always, the shop tonight feels like a social club; beneath the benevolent gaze of Jesus, Nefertiti, and the Reverend King, everyone looks to be having a fine time. Outside, the early winter darkness has fallen like a black curtain against the shop window, but inside Willie's it's bright and warm.

Corey, whistling the theme song to "The Andy Griffith Show," grabs a razor and stands next to Russell, trimming his right sideburn. Corey has always been solicitous of Russell's fashion needs; when Russell started dressing with flair this year, Corey remained in the locker room to troubleshoot in case Russell hit any snags knotting his tie. And now that Russell has let his hair grow back, Corey is making sure it does so in an orderly fashion. "What's up with Terry," he asks.

"I still love her; don't get me wrong," Russell answers solemnly. "But I can't show her that, can't be saying, 'Terry, I love you, I want to be with you.' Maybe she say, 'Russell, I just don't feel that way.' What if she decide she don't want to be with me?" Russell searches Corey's face unhappily. "I would take that hard, I'm telling you. I got to act like I don't care, got to keep myself covered, got to keep her on a long spoon." Lately I have seen, amid Russell's usual stack of SAT review books, a volume called *The Black Man's Guide to the Black Woman.*

"You just got to tease her a little, is all," Corey says authoritatively. He moves behind Russell to trim his neck hairs. "Like, instead of kissing her on the lips? Kiss her on the nose. Then kiss her on the eyebrow. Give her a kiss on the ear. Before you know it, she'll be beggin' you, 'When you gonna kiss me on the *lips?*'" Corey laughs and laughs, confident that his advice has been thoroughly market-tested.

Across the room, I hear Willie Johnson give a snort of disapproval. Willie is cutting Stephon's hair, but mostly he's been keeping a weather eye on his younger brother.

"Whatever you do with Terry," Corey says, moving in front of Russell in order to even off his sideburns, "just don't bust inside her. That almost happened to me."

Hearing this, Willie begins clipping Stephon's hair with growing agitation. "Corey's smart, but he's stupid too," Willie says to me. "You know what I mean? In junior high, he was a virgin with a ninety average. Now he's got a sixty-five. You tell me." I start laughing, but Willie says, "No, I'm *serious*, man. I've been trying to talk to him. I say, 'Don't you want to go to college? Don't you know you got to sacrifice for things you want? Don't you know why no coaches have been coming to visit you yet?'" Willie is going at Stephon's head with angry abandon, and Stephon has sunk low in his chair, hoping to avoid a scalping. "Corey could do his homework one-two-three, but he's on the phone all night talking to girls. I say to him, 'There are always gonna be girls around, brother. Girls will be around until you die.' I say to him, 'You got a personal problem? Just tell me.' But he says, 'No, there's nothing wrong.' 'But why lie to me?' I say. 'I'm your brother. I'm not gonna make you or break you.'" Willie lifts his scissors from Stephon's head and looks across the room at Corey. "Sometimes I just want to hit him."

Willie is giving voice now to everyone's worst fear: namely, that Corey will not only fail to secure his college eligibility, but that he will get one of his girlfriends pregnant. At times, it has seemed that the concern over Corey's dating habits borders on the extreme, but Willie argues that it may not be taken seriously enough. As many Coney Island players have abandoned their college dreams because they became fathers as have those who became drug dealers. Chocolate, for example, left behind a three-week-old baby when he was shot. "Girls and crack," goes the mantra in Coney Island. "Girls and crack." In fact, girls and even the simple distractions of friends are considered such a threat to a college career that the neighborhood's talented athletes are being urged to give up the rights and privileges of adolescence altogether and attend a high school far from home; they will be lonely, but they will keep on the straight and narrow.

Corey's brother Louis took this strategy one step further, deliberately avoiding Lincoln High for the seclusion of a predominantly male school, then spending an extra year at a prep school that serves as a sort of academic rehab clinic for basketball players. Not coincidentally, he passed his SATs and became the first of the six Johnson boys — indeed, one of the first Coney Island players in years — to avoid the juco system and go directly to a Division I school.

Louis Johnson was so dedicated to his craft that he would practice his shot under the Garden lights until four A.M., even in the driving rain. Everyone — not only Willie, but Disco, Mr. Lou, and the rest of the neighborhood — wishes Corey shared his brother's singlemindedness. But Corey's sensibility is much too quirky for that, and I am finally understanding the danger that represents in Coney Island. If Corey lived anywhere else — certainly if he had grown up twenty-five miles north, in one of New York's white suburbs — he would play the offbeat writer whose poor grades and popularity with girls earn him a four-year sentence at a midlevel school like Colgate, to be served while his classmates all go Ivy. In the movie version, Corey would be played with dashing ennui by Matt Dillon or Keanu Reeves, and he would end up in the climactic scene getting the girl *and* a job after he learned to stop slacking off. But Corey fools around in an arena where there is, of course, no such thing as a safety school — nor, for that matter, safety nets of any kind — and where the credits usually roll on far less sanguine endings.

There is, in addition to the grave threat this represents for Corey's future, a sad bit of irony in all of this. Black, inner-city kids are always accused of doing nothing but throwing a ball through a hoop. At least that's what a lot of white suburbanites assume they're doing. Then along comes someone like Corey, who takes pleasure in a million other things. (He may not show up in the morning for first-period class, but Corey will happily stay in school late to dazzle his classmates with his singing and dancing in the annual talent show.) In Coney Island, however, you deviate from the one and only path to college at extreme personal risk — scholarships for athletes being significantly easier to come by than those for underachievers or ghetto poets.

•

By the time Russell and Corey submit themselves to Willie's shears, it's already late, so I agree to drive them back to Coney Island. All three are tired, and we ride along Flatbush Avenue and down Ocean Parkway in a rare moment of peace and quiet. Finally, Russell turns to me and says, "What do you know about Rob Johnson?"

Oh, boy.

Johnson is a street agent, a middleman, a flesh peddler. Worse than any high school or college recruiter, he makes his living by getting chummy with high school players and brokering them to colleges for a fee, though the coaches who pay it swear they've never heard of him. According to the latest allegations, Johnson used to recruit players for the B/C camp, then moved on to bigger fish, getting himself (and Syracuse coach Jim Boeheim, among others) entangled in an NCAA investigation. But Johnson's recent notoriety hasn't kept him from showing up regularly at the Lincoln gym this year — a tall black man with an enormous gut, Day-Glo Nikes, and a thick gold chain around his wrist. Lately Johnson has been attending varsity practice, where he sits alone in the bleachers, then lingers around the star players afterward, offering to drive them home or take them to the movies. He is, I can imagine, an appealing figure to broke and fatherless kids like Russell.

"Has Rob offered to be your agent?" I ask. Russell looks out the window and says, "He called me last night. Said he liked the way I played. A *lot*." I tell Russell he might want to check out Rob's reputation, but Russell says, "It don't matter. I've decided to sign with South Carolina. They really want me. They said they would *love* to sign me." Having surprised us all with this sudden decision, Russell pulls out a paper bag with his customary after-practice snack: a plain bagel and a carton of Tropicana.

"You should at least visit before you make up your mind," Corey advises. He's stretched luxuriously across the backseat. "They're all gonna make it *sound* good."

"But I already know I want to go there," Russell says between mouthfuls.

"Russell, you've never been outside Coney Island! How the hell are you gonna know? Look" — Corey lowers his voice and tries to speak to his best friend in tones of unimpeachable reasonableness — "Russell, say you're gonna marry someone. You gonna marry the first girl you sleep with? No. Of course not. You're gonna look around, see what the other girls can do for you, and then make your decision. Same with colleges. You got to go up there and have a careful look around." Corey is utterly confounding: he's blowing his own talent and won't listen to anyone's warnings, yet he knows exactly what his friend should do and feels obliged to speak his mind. Maybe that's what he gets from this odd friendship with Russell — the chance to say out loud what he himself should do, even if he never takes his own good advice.

"Nobody can make me take visits if I don't want to," Russell protests.

Corey laughs. "Nobody's gonna *make* you do anything. But you might as well let them show you a good time. Let them wine you and dine you. When my recruiting starts, I'm going to have me some *fun*."

Russell, having finished his snack, balls up the paper bag and tosses it out the window with an air of finality. "I don't want to be wined and dined."

As much as he hates Coney Island, Russell has never lived anywhere else, and I know that he fears his dark complexion will get him into trouble outside his home turf. That may explain why he doesn't want to take any recruiting visits. But something else is up. Corey notes this and changes strategy. "What's your reason?" he asks Russell. "You got to have a reason."

"I'm not like everybody else," Russell replies, staring sullenly out the window.

"Yes," Corey says slowly. "This is true."

"Look, all the best players sign in the fall. Only the scrubs wait until spring. April signers is the leftovers."

"I'm not telling you to sign in the spring," Corey says, "I'm just saying you change your mind every day."

Russell twists around to look his friend in the eye. "I'm telling *you*, Corey, I'm having a great season. My stock is going up. I'm gonna be big time. I'm gonna have Big East schools recruiting me just like Tchaka by the end of the year — it'll be funny." Russell is getting worked up now. "And when those schools that lost interest in me, like Rutgers and Duquesne, come back in the spring, I'm gonna be, like, 'So why did you come back *now?*' I'm gonna be, like, 'Too late, *sucka!*' I'm gonna be throwing it on niggers all year! Tomahawk jams! Reverse alley-oops!" Russell starts thrashing about in the front seat, dunking his orange juice carton into the ashtray of my car.

"Man, you are one *crazy* nigger!" Corey says. "I'm not talking about dunking! I'm talking about whether you should sign at some school you never even seen in your life!"

"Don't matter. It's my decision. And part of growing up is learning to live with your decisions. Even if it turns out to be a nightmare."

"But why?"

"Don't push me, Corey."

"But *why?*"

"Because I don't want to talk about it." Russell's voice is rising up the scale.

"That's not a reason."

"Yes it is."

"No it's not."

"BECAUSE I HATE ALL THIS FUCKING RECRUITING!" Russell screams. "All right?"

Corey leans back against his seat, defeated. "Okay, well, at least that's a reason."

Nine

IN EARLY DECEMBER a cold front hit New York City. In Coney Island, the wind coming off the icy Atlantic sped down the canyon of Ocean Parkway, and when the players and I left the school building after practice, it stung our eyes and lashed our cheeks like a whip. Sometimes the players collected by the bus stop outside Lincoln to review the day's events before heading home. As we stood around in the six o'clock darkness, stamping our feet and warming our hands with our breath, I couldn't help noticing how the expansive after-school talk of last spring — about city championships and summer camps — had been reduced to the essentials: which coaches were still calling, which ones had lost interest, how many more opportunities the players had to take the SATs.

And as the gap between Tchaka's fortunes and those of his Coney Island teammates widened, so too did the fault lines that ran just beneath the surface of this team. For a long time I attributed the friction between Tchaka and the Coney Island crew merely to geography. After practice, Russell, Corey, and Stephon often hung out together in Coney Island or at Willie's shop while Tchaka went home to Queens. But among black neighborhoods in New York, I see now that geography speaks to a more delicate issue: social class. "Man, Coney Island is *fucked up*," Tchaka said to me one day. "Out by the projects, it's *crazy*, like another country. I remember I was walking down Surf Avenue once. I saw about forty stringy-haired niggers coming straight at me. I'm looking right and left, figuring where I can run. Then someone I knew from Lincoln came up and rescued me. I thought, 'Thank God. You just saved my life.' Out there all you gotta do is *look* at someone wrong and they want to shoot you. After I get to college, I'm never going into fucking Coney Island again."

In this context, "stringy-haired niggers" sounds like barely disguised code for the disdain, even fear, with which Tchaka views some blacks from the projects; and certain of the Coney Island players readily return the insult, suggesting that the more middle-class players like Tchaka can't play the game the way they do in Coney Island.

"Yo, nigger, what position you gonna play in college?" Stephon asked Tchaka after his Seton Hall trip. The two were getting dressed across the aisle from each other in the Lincoln locker room.

"Forward," Tchaka replied.

"*Power* forward?" Stephon said with mock incredulity.

"Yeah. So?"

"But you're only six-six," said the five-nine Stephon.

"Six-seven, nigger." Tchaka slammed his locker shut.

"You know power forwards got to dribble and shoot," Stephon said, his voice richly condescending. "You been working on that?" Stephon handed Tchaka a paper cup and suggested that Tchaka dispose of it for him.

Tchaka, stuck with the damned cup in his hand, was speechless for a moment. Then he exploded, "You're a *freshman*, man! What the hell is *wrong* with you!"

"I can't wait till you go to college," Stephon said with a sneer. "You'll be carrying luggage." The teammates finished dressing in silence, then they headed home to their separate neighborhoods and their very separate lives.

Most nights when Tchaka arrived in Queens, he came home to an answering machine full of messages from the coaches ("Do you miss me?" Rick Barnes asked) and a stack of mail. One day, Tchaka received letters from all the players on the Villanova team ("Tchaka — Hope to see you in a Wildcat uniform soon!"). Meanwhile reporters at the *New York Daily News, Newsday,* the *Providence Journal-Bulletin,* and Newark, New Jersey's *Ledger Star* were calling Coach Hartstein at school, looking for a scoop on where Tchaka would sign. The Villanova assistant coach John Olive even called *me* at home one night. "Have you heard anything?" he asked. "Did Tchaka say anything about his Seton Hall visit?" I demurred, but the coach pressed on. "I hear Tchaka wasn't in school today. What's his mood been like?" The more I dodged, the more frantic Coach Olive became. "Does Tchaka seem up? What's your gut say? If you had a gun to your head, where would you say he's going to sign?"

From the moment his Seton Hall tour ended, I knew Tchaka was no longer in doubt. For months he refused to get distracted from the things he most wanted to hear and simply waited until a coach finally hit upon them. As the NCAA's early signing deadline approached, the recruiting hysteria grew more intense, but Tchaka remained the calm center of the storm.

"I just want to get it over with," he says one evening at his house in Queens. "I just want it to end so I can go to sleep. Everyone's been telling me not to let all the recruiting go to my head. I'm surprised, with the things everybody says to me, my head's not a lot bigger." An expression of serenity settles over his face. "But I don't really listen to the coaches. They never tell you the truth. They all say how good you are, even when you know you're not playing well. But like Magic Johnson says in his video, 'Never be satisfied with your game.' That's the way I feel. I'm only satisfied with twenty points, twenty rebounds, no turnovers, and catching all my passes."

As he speaks, Tchaka sits on the edge of his bed, his back straight as a rod and his hands cupping his knees. He looks as proper as an altar boy, and his words sound like a recitation. But I see that he is actually still with pensiveness, his gaze directed toward the far shore of his thoughts. "Sometimes I try to think what my dad would tell me about all this — the coaches, the recruiting," he says. "He played basketball for Brooklyn College, you know; was even on TV a couple of times. So he knows what it's like." Tchaka doesn't stir from his straight-backed position; he is almost in a kind of reverie. "My father and I used to play together, back when I just played basketball to play. You know — for the fun. Not like I do now — for the scholarship and stuff. He would talk to me. And I think that's what he would tell me now — to just keep calm about it and not sweat it so much. Just, you know, play the game."

Talking about his father makes Tchaka uncharacteristically shy, for suddenly he leaps from the bed and climbs on a chair and staples back a poster of Larry Johnson that keeps drooping from the wall. But he jumps down just as quickly and signals me — "Yo, c'mere" — to follow him into the living room. He stands in front of a small, framed photograph that looks to be a picture of himself at about the age of ten. "Who's that?" he asks me.

"You, of course."

"Looks just like me, right?" Tchaka removes the frame from the wall to allow me a closer look. "That's my dad when he was a kid." The resemblance between Tchaka and his young father is extraordinary. "My mother says, since he looked exactly like me then, it means I'm gonna grow up to look exactly like him." Tchaka seems pleased at the prospect. He returns the picture to its hook, squaring it with his thumb and forefinger.

Just then his mother walks through the door. "Hello, Precious," she says, giving Tchaka a kiss. "And how are you, Precious," she says, kissing me as well. She drops her bag in the middle of the floor, walks immediately into the kitchen, fills a pot with hot water, and sits down on the living room couch to soak her feet. "I believe this job will kill me," she announces operatically. "Yes, it will! It will strike me right down in the prime of my life!" Then she resumes her normal speaking voice to add, "'Cause it sure ain't makin' me rich." She sighs and props her head on a pillow and explains that she has received some alarming news. Her landlady wants to sell the nicely maintained, one-story house the Shipps are renting, and unless the family can come up with a $6000 down payment within a year to buy it themselves, they will have to find somewhere else to live — back in Bed-Stuy, for example, or the projects.

"I'm very anxious right now because, even with Tracie helping me out, I'm the main supporter and I don't have the money," she says while Tchaka takes a seat at the dining room table, clicks on the TV, and watches a Nike commercial featuring Charles Barkley. "And one of the biggest securities in Tchaka's life right now is this home. There's no riffraff on the streets around here. It's quiet, peaceful. If he didn't have this, he'd go crazy. So we have just got to find a way to keep it." Mrs. Shipp looks at her son for a long moment; he's oblivious of what she's been saying, watching Sir Charles and shoveling dry cereal into his mouth. She smiles. "But now, with the Seton Hall scholarship, at least I can go to sleep each night knowing he's going to get a marvelous education, he'll be in a good environment, and he will grow up to be the excellent young man his father and I always knew he would be. He's really in the time of his life right now." She leans back on the couch and sighs, this time less with fatigue than with relief. "So we have a lot of financial problems. We struggle. But when I look at Tchaka,

I realize we are also blessed." This, truly, is what one hopes for Tchaka and all his teammates — not necessarily that they will become big college stars, where the coaches will continue to lie to them and the players will be lucky to finish their four college years with a diploma in hand, but that basketball will help them get an education in order that they might do something else with their lives besides play ball.

Mrs. Shipp clears her throat. "Tchaka, dear?" she says to her son, speaking now in a girlish, importunate voice. "After you graduate from Seton Hall, dear? And you make all that money in the pros, dear? Will you share it with your hard-working and devoted mother?"

Tchaka looks up from the TV, walks over to the couch, and begins shadow boxing, watching his reflection in the mirror above his mother's head. "Nope," he replies. "I'll buy me some Nikes."

"I mean it," Mrs. Shipp says sternly. "*Will you share it with your mother?*"

Tchaka frowns. "I already told you, no. That dust is mine."

"You *won't?* You're gonna be in the NBA and we're gonna be in a *shelter?*"

"Ma, that's a stupid question," Tchaka says, exasperated. "Of *course* I'll share it with you. What you think I'm gonna do?"

Mrs. Shipp smiles and sighs again and splashes her feet around in the pot. Tchaka starts throwing punches at the living room cabinet.

"Tchaka, dear?" Mrs. Shipp begins again. Tchaka shoots her a look. "Will you let me be your manager?"

"Ma, don't start with that."

"But you're gonna need someone to help you manage all that money."

"I'll manage it myself."

"You'll need a responsible adult."

"What you think *I'll* be when I get all that money?" Now Tchaka begins jumping up and down, palming the ceiling. The basketball trophies on the windowsill shake, and the water at Mrs. Shipp's feet laps over the edge of the pot.

"But you're going to need someone to help you invest it," Mrs. Shipp says.

Still jumping, Tchaka speaks in staccato bursts, as if someone is pounding on his chest. "I'll . . . just . . . take . . . a . . . course . . . in . . . money . . . management." He stops hopping. "Either that or I'll keep my money in a safe under my bed," he says reasonably. "When I need to deposit, I'll deposit. When I need to withdraw, I'll withdraw."

Mrs. Shipp shakes her head. "I think you'll need an expert like me." She fluffs the pillow behind her head. "And I only charge ten percent."

"Ma! What you so hype about?"

"I ain't hype. *You* hype," she answers.

"No, *you* hype!" he yells back.

"No, *you* hype!"

The two of them stare at each other fiercely, waiting for the other to smile.

"Tchaka, dear?"

"What *now!*"

"Get your mother a glass of water."

•

A few nights later, Russell invites me over to his apartment after practice. He still has a few more chances to pass his SATs, but time is running out. And as he continues to struggle with the test, most of the Division I coaches who came to see him in the fall have given up and moved on to other players. That's when the junior colleges, smelling a potential Prop 48 casualty, begin to send out their grim invitations. "We're all hoping you make 700s on your SATs. Let's assume you don't. Come to the sunny Southwest," writes the coach of a community college in Texas, the largest and most competitive junior-college league.

"Man, I hope everything works out," Russell says as we drive down Surf Avenue toward his project. "I hope everything works out like it's supposed to." Deep down, though, he seems to have realized that it doesn't matter how he plays this season or whether he continues to get good grades or stays away from the neighborhood drug dealers or dresses for success or dunks in public — all those items on his long list of "Things to Do to Get My Scholarship." Unless he gets 700 very soon, in the coaches' eyes he will remain easily exchangeable for a player with better test scores.

Coney Island never looks quite so forlorn as it does just before Christmas. The Cyclone and Wonder Wheel have been shuttered for the winter; the boardwalk is littered with broken glass and crack vials. Certain of the neighborhood's urban beach activities continue — guys combing the sand for loose change with their metal detectors and car owners attending to their batteries with solar-powered rechargers. But for the most part the neighborhood is more deserted than ever. Just behind the boardwalk and the amusement park, where the projects rise up, the cold weather has swept the streets clean of everyone but the most hardened criminals. Garbage drifts down empty alleyways like tumbleweed. At night, Christmas lights blink on and off from the top floors of the projects, semaphoring into the ocean darkness, but few people are around to receive the holiday message.

This is my first visit to Russell's home, and as he and I walk into the lobby of his building, he says, his eyes cast down in weariness and shame, "Welcome to the old ghetto." Russell's building is identical in design with the one in which Corey and Stephon live just a block away — fourteen stories of weathered brick sheltering pissy stairwells and dim hallways. I have always assumed it was no better or worse than theirs. But Russell assures me that looks are deceiving. The way he peers around the elevator door before entering makes me believe him.

Upstairs, his family's apartment is oppressively small: a living room, kitchenette, bathroom with walls of peeling brown paint, and two bedrooms. His mother has one; Russell and his two younger sisters, using bunk beds and a cot, share the other. Tonight the temperature outside has dropped to 13 degrees, and with the apartment radiators offering little help, Russell's mother, even in her absence, is heating the place by warming a small brick on the top of the stove. From the top floors of all these projects you can see straight to the amusement park and the Atlantic Ocean beyond. But the vast, unobstructed views serve mostly as reminders of the punitive conditions in which the Thomases and everyone else in this neighborhood live, locked fearfully away behind their steel apartment doors.

I notice that Russell is wearing a new ring on his finger and I ask whether it's a present from Terry; perhaps this means they're back on track. But Russell doesn't answer me. Instead he says, "Want to see some pictures of Terry and me?" He pulls out a scrapbook filled with newspaper clippings about himself and the Lincoln team. Stuffed in the back are a pile of loose snapshots. "We been together a long time," he says wistfully as he looks through the photos and passes them to me one by one. "All those days last summer — picnics, all the stuff we used to do." He lingers over one shot of Terry and him. "Maybe someday — way, way off in the future — we'll get married." Russell and I are still looking at the photos when he hears a key in the front door. Hastily, he grabs the pictures from my hand and shoves them back in the scrapbook, snapping it shut just as his mother walks in.

"You come home right after practice?" she asks anxiously. Russell nods, and she smiles in my direction. "Russell thinks I'm overprotective, but I have to know where he's at. If he's at practice or at Willie's, okay. But just hanging out on the street? No!" She drops a bag of groceries on the kitchen table and lets out a long sigh. The neighborhood's one decent supermarket is fifteen blocks away; any time she needs more than a few items from the store, she has to take a car service there and back. "This is a hard neighborhood. *Wicked*, nothing but drugs out there," says Mrs. Thomas, removing her coat. "Most of Russell's friends are wasting their lives. You've got to have a strong and powerful will not to go in that direction."

Joyce Thomas, I know from my one previous meeting with her, certainly has that. Now she gets to work in her small apartment, unpacking groceries and heating up some baked ziti on the top of her stove. Suddenly a burst of what sounds like machine gun fire erupts outside, scaring me half to death, but Mrs. Thomas doesn't react in any way. "You gotta always watch who you're hanging out with around here," she says warily. "'Cause even if you're doing nothing wrong, you'll end up getting blamed too. I always tell Russell, it takes that much" — she spreads two fingers an inch apart — "to get into trouble, and that much" — now two hands shoulder width apart — "to get out of it." She looks over to her son, but he has vanished from the living room. "So far Russell's okay." She raps twice on her kitchen table. "So far." I start to say something, but Mrs. Thomas cuts me off. "When Russell messes up, I knock him out. I *do*. I tell him, 'Don't you dog me, boy; I'm all you got!'" She is looking at me with great force in her eyes, and I quickly get the feeling that there's more going on here than I yet comprehend. "I don't care how big Russell is or how much ball he plays," she says, still staring at me. "I'll put a ball in his head!"

Soon Russell reappears, this time with his Walkman on and a strange, stricken look on his face. He starts to sing aloud to a slow love song coming from his Walkman, though all we can hear, of course, is Russell's sad crooning.

Suddenly Mrs. Thomas takes in a breath. Looking at Russell, she says, "Did you do it?" Russell keeps on singing, so Mrs. Thomas walks over to him, picks up his hand, and examines the ring. "Terry gave it back to you?"

He slides the headphones around his neck. "I took it back," he says. His voice is clotted.

"How did it go?" his mother asks.

Russell can't think of anything to say. And I'm wondering, *When did all this happen?*

At last Russell murmurs, "She was real sad."

Mrs. Thomas doesn't stir. The apartment is quiet except for the refrigerator's hum. A few moments pass. Russell has begun to turn inward, and the next words he utters seem to reach us from a great distance. "She was crying, hanging on to my leg, saying, 'Don't go, don't go.'"

"Now don't you worry about Terry," Mrs. Thomas says matter-of-factly. "She'll be all right. There are plenty of other Russell Thomases out there. You just watch out for *yourself.*"

"I'm real sad, too," he says quickly, and I can see him struggling not to cry.

"Don't be. How long were you together — five, six months? That's not so hard to get over." Mrs. Thomas turns briskly toward her groceries and continues to unpack. Russell stands stock-still in the middle of the living room, staring at his feet.

She glances over at me. "I explained to Russell, 'You want friends? Fine. But I don't want you attached to *anyone.* You will go to college alone, and so will Terry.'" Russell can't bear to hear his mother's words, so he puts on his Walkman and begins his tone-deaf accompaniment. "A girl like Terry could make him do something stupid," she goes on. "He gets carried away. He's very emotional, you know."

At first I am appalled by Mrs. Thomas's harsh words and seeming indifference to her son's pain, though the more she talks, the easier it is to hear what lies beneath it: a desperation to get Russell away from Coney Island, and a suspicion of anyone who might stand in his way, that are so great, she will do anything she deems necessary, even if it means persuading him to give up the one most stabilizing influence in his life at a time when his need is the greatest.

"Russell got a second chance on this planet," she says, referring to Russell's suicide threat last year, "and no one gets that! *No one!*" She stares at me again, this time with such unblinking intensity that I have to fight the urge to look away. "He's got a lot of decisions ahead of him. Important decisions. *Business* decisions. Without that scholarship, he's nothing. *Nothing!*" Mrs. Thomas looks to her son to gauge his reaction, but Russell has checked out completely. He's turned his Walkman up to full volume, and he's singing as loud as he can.

Ten

THE LINCOLN TEAM'S most important game of the season — and the last one I would watch before my time with the players came to an end — took place right before the Christmas holiday. Abraham Lincoln plays William Grady twice a year, and each game is an all-out war. These are the two schools that sit directly across from each other on Ocean Parkway in Coney Island. They boast the two finest basketball programs in the PSAL, and their meetings are the most highly anticipated and hotly contested in the league. Both schools have reached the city's quarter finals in each of the last six years. Lincoln won the city championship at Madison Square Garden last year; Grady won it the year before. And the two schools have traded off their division title every year but one since it was established almost ten years ago. Perhaps the most memorable Lincoln-Grady game took place in 1986, when Lincoln snatched a one-point victory after Dwayne (Tiny) Morton stole a Grady inbounds pass with five seconds left, directly in front of Villanova's Rollie Massimino, Duke's Mike Krzyzewski, and Maryland's Lefty Driesell. (He still ended up, like most of his teammates, having to attend a junior college.)

Since most of the Lincoln and Grady kids come from the same Coney Island projects, and a few players are also related to each other, their games serve as an extension of the great summer playground contests at the Garden — neighbor plays neighbor, cousin guards cousin, and, as Disco once put it, "the bragging rights of Coney Island are at stake." Among the players, the Lincoln-Grady rivalry is considered a friendly affair. Not among the coaches. At Grady, they often snicker about how few of Bobby Hartstein's players ever make it to four-year schools. "They say *my* players never go to college?" Hartstein retorts. "Who's the most successful guy ever to graduate from Grady? The guy who invented axle grease?" For a while, in fact, Hartstein and the head Grady coach, Jack Ringel, did not speak to each other. And in large part because Jock McMahon, Ringel's assistant, was recruiting so many Coney Island athletes who at one time would automatically have enrolled at Lincoln, Hartstein hadn't had the satisfaction of beating Ringel in three seasons. The last five games in the series had all gone to Grady.

At the team meeting in a Lincoln classroom an hour before tip-off, Hartstein makes his way through the Grady roster, trying to determine the various skills of the opposing players. Pacing back and forth in front of his team, Hartstein goes through all the starters, getting the local scouting reports. "What about Ronald Cromer?" he asks. "Can he shoot?"

"Oh, yeah," says Stephon, sitting in the first row of desks. "He can hit it."

"And Lorenzo?"

"He's got a shot," Stephon replies. "But not from deep."

Throughout the meeting, the team managers, told to keep an eye on things in the Lincoln gym, keep returning with news from the front. The Grady team has arrived and is downstairs changing in the weight room . . . such a crush of people have come to watch the game that both bleachers are already full . . . there's even a rumor that Spike Lee, the Brooklyn-based film impresario, has called the school to reserve a ticket. ("Must be coming in his capacity as

Stephon's agent," someone jokes.) Each time a manager comes or goes, Hartstein barks at the player sitting closest to the door to keep it shut. Soon a group of Lincoln students is crowding in the hallway, peering through the classroom window at the team's star players. But Russell, Corey, Tchaka, and Stephon sit calmly while their coach tries to walk off his excess energy. "The kids aren't very emotional, are they?" Neil Steinberg, one of Hartstein's assistant coaches, whispers to me. "Bobby's nervous though. He won't admit it, but have you seen him sit any time in the last half-hour? You could say, 'Bobby, someone just died on the court.' He'd say, 'Is that right?' and keep on talking." At times like this, I have trouble aligning my current image of Hartstein with the low-key father figure he seemed eight months ago. But I realize that he is no less devoted to his players now than he was back then; he just seems, like every coach I have met, also devoted to winning.

At last, having worked his way through the Grady roster, Hartstein comes to the opposition's one truly great player: Maurice (Fresh) Brown, their extraordinary senior point guard who played alongside Tchaka and Russell at the Empire State Games and has recently signed with Saint John's University. As all the Coney Island players know from having grown up with Maurice — he lives in the Carey Gardens project, eight blocks from Corey, Russell, and Stephon — he can destroy a team in two ways: with his deadly three-point shooting or, if he is allowed to keep his dribble alive, by penetrating the defense and creating easy shots for his teammates. However, if Lincoln can separate Maurice from the ball, denying him the chance to shoot or pass, Grady would have to rely on its other, inferior weapons. Hartstein decides that Russell will guard Maurice; with that one move, the game is put almost entirely in his hands.

With twenty minutes to go before tip-off, I walk into the Lincoln gym. The place is filled to capacity. So many students and teachers from both Lincoln and Grady have crowded onto the bleachers that all subsequent arrivals are told to find a place on the gym floor behind each basket. Little kids are standing at the door, yelling to their older brothers, "Yo, can you get me in?" The noise, even at conversational pitch, is overwhelming; I feel it rumbling inside my chest. And when I scan the bleachers, I realize that just about all of them are there — all the people I have got to know over the past eight months with the Lincoln team: the high school sports reporter for *Newsday*, a scout from the most influential talent report on the East Coast, Disco, Mr. Lou, Willie Johnson, Donald Marbury, Joyce Thomas, the street agent Rob Johnson, and several generations of past Coney Island players — the few who went away to college and are home for Christmas break, and the many more who never left the neighborhood and have nothing else to do on a weekday afternoon but show up at their old school to watch a game.

Over by the Lincoln bench, Coach Hartstein is airing his familiar grievances about alleged recruiting violations at Grady. "It's really a disgrace," he says to his assistants. "One kid just got kicked out of his old high school, another never shows up for school, and I heard they got some South American player in his sixth year in high school. We should make them submit their names to the eligibility committee." Just then, Jock McMahon walks over to Hartstein for the obligatory pregame greeting. He says, "Good luck," and shakes Hartstein's hand, but neither man will look the other in the eye.

When I catch up with the Lincoln players again, they have already dressed in their blue and white uniforms and are gathered at the head of the stairs that lead from the basement locker room up to the gym door. In previous months the players would stand here, nervously shifting from one foot to the other, waiting for their opposition to arrive on court. Then they would carefully arrange them-selves in a row, fling open the door, and make their big entrance by splitting into two lines and sprinting opposite ways around the court while the other team watched and the crowd went wild. But Grady is still getting changed in the weight room, and no one is in the mood for such adolescent antics anyway. "Just run out, man," Russell says impatiently. "It doesn't matter. Let's just go out."

"Yeah, it's just another game," Stephon says. "Let's go to work." And so they do.

As soon as the ball goes up, Tchaka gets his first dunk, Stephon hits a three, and before I know it, Lincoln has jumped to a 7-0 lead. But just as quickly the momentum shifts the other way as Maurice Brown, shaking off Russell with picks and screens, organizes an efficient Grady counterattack. By the end of the first quarter, the score is tied at 16 each, the crowd is growing more hysterical, and it looks as if we're in for a long afternoon.

As the second quarter begins, Lincoln seems to convert each time downcourt. So does Grady, though, and the score climbs in equal increments. With five minutes to go in the quarter, Grady ekes out a 23-22 lead, and I realize we have now arrived at a crucial moment — not only the first time Lincoln has fallen behind in this game, but the first time all season the team has lost a lead this far into a game. And Maurice, like all great players, knows how to capitalize on his psychological advantage. In quick succession he dumps four three-pointers on the Lincoln team, saving the final indignity for last, when he launches from well beyond NBA range with one second left in the half. In sixteen minutes of playing time, Maurice has scored 20 points, and the Grady players trot into the locker room with a 40-33 lead.

At halftime, Russell, Corey, Stephon, Tchaka, and their teammates sit on the stairs just outside the gym. Hartstein takes up position on the landing below, where he can pace and look up at his team. He is silent for a minute, and the only sound in the echoing hallway is his footfall and the players' heavy breathing. Then the coach explodes. "Russell, you're supposed to be guarding Maurice and he's hit *nine* threes in your face!" he screams. "You're wasting your time trying to guard him! You're a disgrace! You can't guard *anybody!*" Russell, his head between his shoulder blades, doesn't stir. "You don't listen; you don't pay attention. We said Maurice is not to shoot a three. He's got nine threes in the half." Hartstein looks around at the rest of his players. "No one is rebounding! No one is moving without the ball! No one is playing any defense whatsoever! Whenever Maurice drives, no one helps out on defense — you all stand around watching!" Getting no argument from his players, Hartstein lowers his voice. "All right, this is what we're gonna do. We're gonna form a box-and-one defense — four players in a zone, and Russell, you just stay on Maurice wherever he goes." Russell looks up now, his face drained of expression. "You don't help out on any other coverage, okay? You just stay on Maurice. Don't let him shoot the ball. Don't let him even *touch* the ball. You got it?" Russell nods. The players climb to their feet and trudge back out to the court.

The second half begins, and Russell gets to work right away. He hits back-to-back three-pointers, bringing Lincoln to within one, and the whole team seems to shake off its torpor at once. The key to Lincoln's offense all season has been the fast break. Most high school coaches avoid run-and-gun ball in favor of a disciplined half-court offense. But the extraordinary confluence of Tchaka, Russell, Corey, and Stephon on one team was like a force of nature, impossible to resist. So Hartstein had built this year's varsity into a simulacrum of the great UNLV–Running Rebels teams of yore. After every opponent's shot now, missed or made, Lincoln runs the break.

This is how it works. Tchaka inbounds the ball to Steph-on, who flies down center court while Russell and Corey fill the outside lanes. If Stephon sees that either wingman has a clear path to the hoop, he looks one way, passes the other, and Lincoln gets an easy two. If the initial break is covered, Stephon keeps his dribble alive while Russell and Corey finish their sprint, then turn in at the baseline, running directly past each other beneath the basket. Usually in the traffic and confusion this creates, one of them loses his man and emerges at the opposite corner, free for a three-point chance. If Russell and Corey are still covered, Stephon can pull up for a jump shot himself or wait for Tchaka, trailing down the middle for a thunderous jam. That's six differ-ent scoring opportunities in under ten seconds, and with Stephon leading the charge and making the right split-sec-ond decision almost every time downcourt, the chances of putting some points on the scoreboard are very, *very* good.

And now, with Russell chasing Maurice all over the court, the Grady offense begins to falter. Maurice dodges this way and that, trying to work his way back into the game, but Russell won't stop harassing him. When Maurice has the ball, Russell plants one hand on his back and keeps jabbing the air with the other until Maurice gives up possession. When Maurice is moving without the ball, Russell never leaves his side and keeps flapping his arms like a maniac, making it impossible for his man to receive a pass. This works precisely as Hartstein had hoped. The other Grady players struggle to score and, in their frustrated attempts to get the ball back to Maurice, commit foolish turnovers. The Lincoln fast-break is hard enough to defend against after a made basket; activated by an opponent's turnover, it occurs like a bad dream — swift and irrevocable. At the end of the third quarter, Lincoln has scored 22 points and held Grady to 8 and they go into the huddle, leading 55–48. During the time-out, Hartstein, evidently pleased by his team's performance, says little, except to whisper in Stephon's ear, "Russell's on fire. Look for him."

Back on the court, Russell goes on a rampage. Stephon gets him the ball and Russell hits a three. Stephon feeds him again and Russell shoots one off the dribble. Now Russell goes one on one in the lane and banks it off the glass. Tchaka heaves a full-court pass, and Russell, alone under the basket, honors his vow: he flushes the ball with two hands, giving the backboard a seismic jolt, and the crowd is on its feet, chanting, "Here we go, Lincoln! Here we go!" With two minutes left in the game, Lincoln is up, 78–64, but Russell still won't let poor Maurice touch the ball. And each time he runs downcourt after scoring a basket himself, Russell looks anxiously toward Hartstein, certain he has committed some new and unforgivable sin.

The game is punctuated in the final moments when Russell pulls down a rebound and feeds the outlet to Stephon. Stephon dribbles through a two-player trap until he reaches half court. From there, Stephon spots Tchaka downcourt, the Grady defense beat yet again. Stephon lobs the ball to Tchaka, who could go up for an easy dunk. Instead, Tchaka spins around so that he is facing all his teammates and with his tongue lolling out of his mouth, flushes the ball over his head for one final, triumphant reverse jam. This is too much for the crowd to bear. Everyone starts stamping on the bleachers. A couple of Lincoln students jump onto the court and perform a manic dance. "Man, I *love* the way Russell play!" cries one of the team's freshmen. In the last seconds, Stephon holds the ball at center court until time runs out, then throws it high into the air.

All told, Lincoln has scored 55 points in the second half — a staggering total for a high school game with only eight-minute quarters — and the final ledger reads 88–73. Russell led five Lincoln players in double figures with 23 points, which is, astonishingly, a slightly subpar performance for

him on the offensive end. But he has also done this: throughout the second half, he held Maurice Brown completely score-
less until only 1:40 remained on the clock and victory was
assured. After the game, the *Newsday* reporter pushes through
the deafening crowd to get some comment from Maurice on
why the Grady game plan fell apart. Maurice, ever gracious,
smiles and shakes his head. "Russell Thomas," he says, "is
a *great* defensive player."

In the locker room, the Lincoln players are dancing around.
Some of the younger guys have removed their jerseys and
wrapped them around their heads like turbans. "Three years
we been waiting for this!" they yell. But the Lincoln starters
— the seniors and Stephon — are the first to break away
from the group and return to their lockers. Surprised by
this — I'll never forget Stephon going nuts last summer
when he threw that full-court alley-oop pass to Corey at the
Garden — I join Stephon and ask why he isn't celebrating.
"Oh, that feeling only lasts about four minutes now," he
answers quickly, throwing on his street clothes. "Then it's
back to usual."

I walk over to Russell, alone at his corner locker. "Con-
gratulations," I say, offering my hand. "You played mag-
nificently."

"Yeah?" Russell looks up, genuinely surprised.

"Well, how do you think you played?"

"All right, I guess," he replies, and I know better than to
argue with him.

I go back over to the younger guys, who are replaying
every lovely moment of this game. A few minutes later, I
spot Russell in street clothes, throwing his book bag over
his shoulder and heading up the stairs. He has — just as he
did at the Empires — single-handedly won another game. In
this case, it is the biggest game of the PSAL season, arguably
the finest high school basketball game I have seen this year.
Having just driven himself beyond most limits of hu-

man performance, he leaves the school building looking exhausted, defeated, like a factory worker at the end of a long shift.

•

My time with the Lincoln team has come to an end. After the NCAA banned me from all the Big East campuses, I saw no point in trying to accompany any of the players on their recruiting visits. Besides, now that Tchaka has signed with Seton Hall, there aren't many recruiters interested in the remaining seniors.

Then, one day right before the Christmas holiday, I ran into Mr. Marbury. I hadn't spoken to him since my discussions with the NCAA, so I told him about the organization's ruling: that if I struck a deal with any Lincoln player's family, the kid would lose his eligibility to play college ball. A moment or two passed as he took in the information. "Oh, you got so many angles, don't you!" he cried furiously. "First it's your reporter's rules. Now it's the NCAA, is it? Let's just forget it. Let's just forget the whole thing!" He pushed by me and stormed away.

And a few days after my final conversation with Mr. Marbury, Russell came up to me in the school corridor and told me, haltingly and with great embarrassment, that his mother had ordered him not to speak to me anymore. Apparently, Russell said, she didn't think it wise for him to spend time with a reporter while his recruiting hung in the balance. Confused by this, and unable to get much of an explanation from Russell, I called Mrs. Thomas that night. She sounded angry — not at me so much as at the diminishing possibilities for her son. "What's he going to say to you anyway?" she yelled into the phone. "He's just a poor black boy growing up in a place with a lot of crack and cocaine! Coney Island is like any other place in the world — it's got people on drugs. Thank God he's not on drugs. Thank God he wants something else. But what's he gonna say? That he's got friends wasting away their lives? You don't dog nobody. 'Cause you never know when *you're* gonna fall! I'm just praying to God that he goes to college and gets his diploma and gets out of here. I want him to have what I *never* got. Russell is my only son in this world and I'll do anything in my power to see that he goes the right way. People, they come down to Coney Island and they look at the boardwalk and all the rides and they say, 'Isn't that nice?' And then they see all those buildings behind them and they say, 'Gee, do people *live* back there?' Yeah, well, we live back here. There are people *back* here. There are lives going on *here.* Just because we're black doesn't mean we're stupid . . ."

•

A few nights later, Tchaka is out at Seton Hall to watch a game and meet some of his future teammates. Russell, Stephon, Corey, and I are in my car, making the usual run to Willie's. For months now, Tchaka has been sitting in the locker room at Lincoln or touring the Big East campuses, watching his future fall into place. The Coney Island guys drive around endlessly in my car, in danger of going nowhere. Stephon announces that he's going to get an X shaved into the back of his scalp. Russell is considering a center part like Larry Johnson's. As we approach the barbershop, we pass by a bunch of guys yelling on a street corner. Corey looks at them suspiciously and says, "What are these uglies making so much noise for?" He glances at his friends. "Don't be wasting time at Willie's, all right?" he says. When I ask why, he tells me a gang from a nearby project has been roaming lately. Last week a woman was hit by a stray bullet right outside the shop, so they all want to get their cuts and be gone.

To me, Coney Island's desolate project walkways and stairwells have always seemed more threatening than the raucous street life here along Flatbush Avenue. And, in fact, not only Tchaka but the two other Lincoln players who live across town have now renounced all visits to Coney Island. But Russell, Corey, and Stephon make it clear to me that as they move through the patchwork of neighborhoods that make up Brooklyn, it matters less how bad an area is than if they find themselves outside their own turf; a group of black teenagers (even celebrity basketball players like themselves, fresh from their victory over Grady) will always be at physical risk on foreign soil. Wherever they go, the three scan the streets to see who may be coming up to them. One of their teammates was shot in the hand a few months ago — caught in crossfire in a Crown Heights playground. After spending seven unattended hours in a hospital emergency room, he has just about lost his ability to shoot the ball. Another classmate was shot at a house party recently; he's still in intensive care. "Something's happening, boy, every day, every day," says Russell.

As planned, they're in and out of Willie's in a flash and happy to be heading home. Driving down Mermaid Avenue, I bring up my last conversation with Mr. Marbury, wondering what the players will think of our exchange. Corey laughs and says, "We got all types in Coney Island — the sane, the insane, and the everything in between. We got room for everyone. But you got to open up a dictionary to find the words for them. That's for sure."

"Nah, he just wants to know what's in it for him," Stephon says of his father. "He knows you don't get something for nothing. He knows if you write about the Marburys you're gonna make a lotta loot." Stephon rolls his thumb and forefinger together. "'Cause everybody knows about the Lincoln tradition and wants to read about us."

"What you mean?" Corey says. "No one reads books anymore."

"Then why is Darcy writing about us?"

"'Cause he just wants to write," Corey replies on my behalf. "I know what that's like."

"Then he's a fool," Stephon concludes.

Russell has been in a particularly foul mood all evening, saying little and leaning into the car heater with his thin winter coat, trying to stay warm; it is, if possible, colder now than it was the other night at his apartment. I mention my recent phone conversation with his mother, wondering whether there's a chance she will change her mind. But Russell says, "You don't understand. My mother's *crazy!*"

Stephon pipes in with some advice for me. "Just greet Russell's mother at the door and hit her with a hundred. She'll change her mind." He snickers knowingly. "She's no different than my father. He wants to make sure he gets some of that loot."

At first I think Stephon is missing the point — that Mrs. Thomas's suspicion of me and her desperation to get Russell out of Coney Island are entirely different from Mr. Marbury's demand for money. But Corey sees the connection. "Damn," he says, "your parents must have had a hard life."

"Still do," Stephon replies. "Your father got himself a whole plumbing business. My father and Russell's mother got nothing." Stephon looks at me out of the corner of his eye and says, "You're thinking, *What a bunch of niggers.* Right?"

The word hangs in the air. I can't think of a thing to say. For months I've heard them call each other that, but by putting the word in *my* mouth, Stephon means something far more corrosive by it now.

"You got to think like a black man," Stephon goes on. "Got to learn how to say 'Fuck it, fuck everybody, *fuck the whole damn thing.'* Now *that's* life in the ghetto."

"It's true!" Russell exclaims, his mood improving for the first time all evening. "My mother *is* a nigger! She's a black woman who does not give a damn."

So that's the definition? Someone whose many hard years in an abandoned ghetto have forced her to rely only on herself and have made her suspicious of anyone — Terry, me — who might interfere with her son's tenuous passage out of poverty? Any white parent who did that would be called overprotective, but no matter. Mr. Marbury supplies another definition: someone in urgent need who strives to protect himself from those who would exploit him and to turn the meager resources at his command into something that might support a family. That, as they say at the Nike all-American camp, is what American entrepreneurship is all about. Except, evidently, in the American ghetto.

"Man, I'm *tired* of all this shit!" Stephon slams his hands down hard on his book bag. "Somebody's *got* to make it, somebody's *got* to go all the way. How come this shit only happens to us Coney Island niggers?" He shakes his head wildly and laughs. "My father and Russell's mother — yeah, they're crazy, but it's about time there was a little something for the niggs."

"Something for the niggs!" Russell repeats the line with a hoot. "Yeah, Steph! Time to get outspoken!"

"You got it," Stephon says, and laughs again. Then Corey joins in. And they're all three whooping and slapping their knees — laughing at their parents and, I imagine, at me and at the absurdity of this whole situation.

The coaches point to kids like Tchaka as proof that the system works. But he is the exception — representative not of the 500,000 or so male high school basketball players in this country, but of the *less than 1 percent* of them who will win a Division I scholarship. And Tchaka succeeds in this game not because he is the first kid to work hard and play by the rules. Russell, Corey, and Stephon do that. They stay in school — though their school hardly keeps its end of the bargain. They say no to drugs — though it's the only fully employed industry around. They don't get into trouble with the NCAA — though its rules seem designed to foil them, and the coaches who break the rules usually go unpunished.

Of course none of them is perfect. Russell panics about his SATs and the choices he must make, and has trouble owning up to it. Corey won't apply himself and kids himself into thinking it won't matter. Stephon has — what shall we call it? — an attitude that needs some adjustment. But they operate in an environment that forgives none of the inevitable transgressions of adolescence and bestows few second chances.

Which makes this process of playing for a scholarship not the black version of the American dream, as I had thought eight months earlier, but a cruel parody of it. In the classic parable you begin with nothing and slowly accrue your riches through hard work in a system designed to help those who help themselves. Here, at seventeen years of age, you begin with nothing but one narrow, treacherous path and then run a gauntlet of obstacles that merely reminds you of how little you have: recruiters pass themselves off as father figures, standardized tests humiliate you and reveal the wretchedness of your education, the promise of lucrative NBA contracts reminds you of what it feels like to have nothing in this world.

Jou-Jou, Silk, Chocolate, Spoon, Spice, Ice, Goose, Tiny, T, Stretch, Space, Sky: all of them great Coney Island players, a few surviving all right, but most of them waiting vainly for a second chance, hanging out in the neighborhood, or dead. And here come Russell, Corey, and Stephon in my car, riding down Mermaid toward the projects in the bone chill and gloom of this dark December night, still laughing about "the niggs," hoping for the best, and knowing that in this particular game failure is commonplace, like a shrug, and heartbreak the order of the day.

Afterword: Twelve Years Later

In the years that have passed since they played together in Coney Island, Stephon Marbury, Corey Johnson, Tchaka Shipp, and Russell Thomas have lived lives filled with extravagant success and bitter disappointment, lives whose trajectories seem largely to have been shaped by the events and circumstances of their youth.

Defying the odds and the legacy of his older brothers, Stephon Marbury went on to excel at every level of the game. A member of the U.S. Junior Olympic team that won a gold medal in Argentina in 1994, and *Parade* magazine's High School Player of the Year in 1995, he spent just one year in college — at Georgia Tech University — before entering the 1996 pro draft, where he was picked fourth overall. Now in his eighth season as a pro, he has played with the Minnesota Timberwolves, the New Jersey Nets, the Phoenix Suns, and the New York Knicks. With a career average thus far of 20.4 points and 8.2 assists per game, Stephon, now twenty-six, is only the second player in NBA history (after Oscar Robertson) to average more than 20 points and 8 assists per game. He is also a two-time NBA all-star. In January 2004, the Knicks committed to Stephon's $104.9 million contract that runs through 2009.

Corey Johnson is still brimming with creative and unconventional ideas, even as he operates with a far smaller margin for error than his famous younger cousin. Corey fell ten points short of a 700 on his high school SATs and went to a junior college in Texas. There, many of the fears harbored for him by his friends and family came to pass when he fathered a child, failed several classes, lost his eligibility, and dropped out of school. Over the years, living back in Brooklyn, Corey has had dozens of jobs —working for his father's plumbing business, doing store decorating and occasional modeling — and staying at times just one step ahead of eviction. Nonetheless, he has kept sight of the goal he first nurtured for himself in high school: to become a writer. After four and a half years of work, Corey, now twenty-nine, has finished a book manuscript of "inspirational poetry and memoir," which he is hoping to publish. "I've been down and out, living paycheck to paycheck, in need of help," he says, "but I gotta have faith things are going to work out. Sometimes I can't sleep . . . I can just smell the opportunities."

Tchaka Shipp left high school for Seton Hall University as one of the nation's top recruits, but his dream of playing in the pros quickly began to slip away. Despite Coach P. J. Carlesimo's recruiting promises of ample playing time, Tchaka spent the next two years languishing on the Pirates' bench, averaging three points and three rebounds in just thirteen minutes of action per game. Frustrated by his secondary role and bridling under what he calls Carlesimo's "verbal abuse," Tchaka transferred to the lower-level University of California at Irvine, looking for a starting spot. He was never able to set foot on the Irvine court. In the summer of 1994, just after moving to the West Coast, Tchaka was driving back to campus one night after a long day of practice when he fell asleep at the wheel. His car, a convertible, jumped a center divider, hit a tree, flipped over, and skidded two hundred yards. By the time paramedics arrived, Tchaka, trapped in the wreckage, had no heartbeat or pulse. For the next nine days, he lay in a coma with myriad injuries to his skull, lungs, and legs, along with severe swelling of the part of the brain that controls memory. Eventually he regained consciousness and underwent months of intensive cognitive and physical therapy, returning to school just six months later. By all accounts, he is lucky to be alive. But he has never functioned in the classroom or on the basketball court at his pre-accident level. In 1996, after struggling academically and losing a year of eligibility, he transferred again, this time to a Division II school — C. W. Post on Long Island, New York — where he lost his starting position to ongoing problems with catching and balance. After graduating from C. W. Post in 1998, Tchaka tried out for the Salina Rattlers, a semi-pro team in Kansas, but with a left knee only half as strong as the right, he failed to make the final cut. "It hurts to know that a lot of guys in my class are now in the NBA," he says. "Life is harsh. I've decided not to waste any more time with basketball. I'm just working, trying to stay above water." Now twenty-nine, Tchaka lives with his fiancée and his two-year-old son in Las Vegas, where he does building maintenance, plumbing, and electrical work for $8.50 an hour.

Russell Thomas never gave up hope of riding his basketball prowess to a four-year college degree and a career in nursing. In the spring of his senior year in high school, Russell signed with Philadelphia's Temple University, whose team has regularly been among the nation's top twenty. But on his final SAT attempt, his score went down, Temple withdrew its scholarship offer, and Russell ended up at a junior college near Los Angeles. There, for the next two years, Russell became one of the most electrifying scorers in the junior college leagues, averaging 32 points per game and setting the state community college scoring record with 1,991 career points. Once again, dozens of Division I coaches came to recruit him. This time, wary of their promises, Russell turned down all their offers and accepted a scholarship at the University of California at Riverside, a Division II school, where he thought he would study better and be sure to earn his bachelor's degree. Russell did graduate, earning a degree in sociology in 1996, while his mother and the Johnson brothers looked on. But familiar troubles soon dogged him. While still in college, Russell married, and within a year he was arrested for allegedly striking and pushing his wife. Two years later, he pled guilty in a separate incident to spousal abuse and received two years' probation and an order to attend anger management counseling. "While I was still playing basketball, I was miserable," Russell wrote in a letter to the *Press-Enterprise* newspaper in Riverside, California. "The pressure of living up to people's expectations of going to the pros was unbearable. When I stopped playing basketball, I found myself excluded by others. I was portrayed only as an athlete, nothing else." After college, Russell started attending church regularly and enrolled briefly at the Claremont School of Theology before dropping out and beginning to minister to the homeless in Riverside. Over the next few years, Russell lost touch not only with his wife and young son in California but also with friends and family back in Coney Island. Without a home or job, he began traveling the Southern California coast, collecting aluminum cans for redemption, helping other homeless men and women, and living in tents and cardboard shelters. On the morning of January 18, 1999, in an incident that many believe was intentional, Russell was walking along some train tracks next to the beach in San Clemente, listening to his Walkman, when he was struck from behind by an Amtrak passenger train. He was thrown seventy-five feet and died instantly. He was twenty-six years old.

— D.F.
January 2004, New York City

ACKNOWLEDGMENTS

I could never have written this book without the help of Corey Johnson, Stephon Marbury, Tchaka Shipp, and Russell Thomas, who for almost a year welcomed me into their lives with warmth and enthusiasm; I am greatly indebted to them. I would also like to express my gratitude to the coaching staff at Abraham Lincoln High School and to the many former players and basketball aficionados on Coney Island who showed me around the neighborhood and shared its lore.

Many friends and colleagues also helped during this project. Pamela Kogut was immeasurably generous with her inspiration and support. Ilena Silverman, my editor at *Harper's Magazine*, lent her heart and soul to this book as if it were her own. Paul LeVine and Jake Lamar read several drafts and tirelessly gave of their wisdom, guidance, and friendship. Michael Pollan, Gerald Marzorati, and Lewis Lapham, also of *Harper's*, offered shrewd editorial counsel, as did John Homans of *Details*. Joseph Nocera gave an incisive reading of an early draft. Frances Apt copyedited the manuscript with great care. John Hassan provided expert fact checking. My agent, Flip Brophy, never lost faith, even when my own faith wavered. Eric Friedman was a devoted friend. My mother and sister were encouraging throughout. And I owe a special debt to my book editor, Richard Todd, who set me to it and saw me through it — with grace and good humor all the way.